UNDER YOUR NOSE

Great Philadelphia Sports Stories You've Never Heard

BY MATT LEON

UNDER YOUR NOSE
Great Philadelphia Sports Stories You've Never Heard

ISBN: 978-1-1935592-90-7

Digital Composition by Ilene Griff Design

The following individuals and organizations generously gave permission to reproduce photographs in this book:

INDIVIDUALS: Jason Minick, Greg Carroccio, Mike McLaughlin, Michael Branscomb, The Shirley Family, Harvey Levine, Steve Allen

ORGANIZATIONS: Philadelphia University Athletics, Ursinus College Athletics, Temple University Athletics, Villanova Media Relations, Delaware Valley College Athletics, Philadelphia Flyers, West Chester University Athletics, University of Pennsylvania Athletics

Sports Challenge Network
Philadelphia, PA 19102
267-847-9018
www.sportschallengenetwork.com
email: elik@sportschallengenetwork.com

For Mom and Dad,
who have always been there for me

Introduction

S o why write a book? Wow. If I had a nickel for every time I have been asked that. Actually I don't think I've ever been asked that, but anyway, I'll tell you why — because it's my book and I want to.

I was not hired as the "sports feature" guy back in 2002 when I came on board at KYW Newsradio. I wanted to do sports in addition to my primary news duties, but we already had a crack staff taking care of the major goings on in the city. I had to look for other sports stories that weren't in the headlines or drawing daily attention. In doing that over the years I have stumbled across some fascinating people, stories and events and I am constantly amazed that they haven't gotten more attention when they are sitting right there "Under Your Nose" (Shameless Title Plug). This is a collection of some of them.

Is this a definitive collection? Absolutely not. I'm sure there are countless other great stories waiting to be told that I have yet to come across, and also great stories that have come down the lane that fell into someone else's lap and I didn't have the privilege to cover. I look at this as a sort of cross-section of the sports landscape that plays out in relative obscurity in the Delaware Valley. Some represent incredible success, some are uplifting, some are just representative of the fun that can happen at any given time anywhere in the world of sports.

What do I hope to accomplish with this book? I hope that after you're done reading this you have a greater appreciation for the countless athletes and coaches who put in endless hours for 1/1000th of the attention that we lavish on the "big-time" athletes, coaches and teams. I hope you come away thinking, "I can't believe I haven't heard about that before." And in a time when it seems we as a sports nation have become increasingly critical and jaded, some of these stories will help remind us all why we started to watch and enjoy sports in the first place.

I also have to add that I've been very lucky over the years to cover some great events and do some really cool things because of my various jobs in radio. But without question, putting together this book has been the most fulfilling professional experience of my career. I've learned, laughed and become a better journalist and person through this journey and am very proud of the final product. I can only hope you enjoy reading it half as much as I enjoyed putting it together. So get to it!!

Acknowledgments

This book would not be possible without the help of several people. First, a big shout-out to publisher Eli Kowalski and everyone at Sports Challenge Network Publishing for taking a chance on this project. (When I couldn't get a sniff with anyone and barely got a rejection letter from some companies.)

I'd also like to thank my boss at KYW Newsradio, Steve Butler, for allowing me to have the creative freedom all these years to pursue the stories that have eventually made up this book.

Special thanks to my friend Amy Schneeman for her proofreading skills, so that the original drafts of most of these stories didn't look like they had been put together by a second grader for whom English was a second language.

I picked the brains of several accomplished authors at the beginning and throughout this process who graciously (and in some cases without knowing me previously or simply in passing) provided insight, direction and advice on how to go about putting this whole thing together. They are Sam Carchidi, Larry Kane, Tony Moss, Mark Bowden, Lou Prato, Mark Brennan and Rich Westcott.

Lots of thanks to go around to all the Sports Information Directors and Media Coordinators who helped me during various stages of this project, including setting up interviews, gathering photos, fact-checking, etc. These people excel at one of the planet's more thankless jobs and do it with a smile. This final project would not have been possible without the following people:

Kevin Bonner, formerly of Temple University
(now at La Salle University)

Aimee Cicero, formerly at Temple University
(now with Philadelphia Union)

Derek Crudele, Widener University

Eric Dolan, University of Pennsylvania

Chas Dorman, formerly of the University of Pennsylvania
(now at Lebanon Valley College)

Larry Dougherty, Temple University

Martin Fleming, The TakeDown Report

Greg Gornick, Chestnut Hill College

Paul Gornowski, Holy Family University

Zack Hill, Philadelphia Flyers

Dean Kenefick, Villanova University

Matt Levy, Delaware Valley College

Mike Mahoney, University of Pennsylvania

Lenn Margolis, Cheyney University

Michael Preston, Philadelphia 76ers

Sarah Punderson, Philadelphia University

Kyle Serba, North Carolina Central University

Joe Siville, Philadelphia Flyers

Brian Smith, Philadelphia Flyers

Mike Thornton, Comcast-Spectacor

John Tomsich, Drexel University

Jim Trdinich, Pittsburgh Pirates

Brian Tsao, New York Red Bulls

Jim Wagner, Ursinus College

Acknowledgements

Jen Werner, University of Pennsylvania

Jim Zuhlke, West Chester University

And finally, a special thanks to Susie Brown for her constant support and for not caring when I spent hours in front of the computer screen! On our first date I actually joked about how I was writing a book and how I was on step 4 of 800. Well we just hit 800!! Thank you for being you and I love you!

Table of Contents

Herb Magee has more career wins than any coach in Division II men's basketball history.

Herb Magee

"When I got involved in the coaching part, I knew that I loved it and that I would definitely do this for the rest of my life."

– HERB MAGEE

They say you only get one chance to make a first impression. The thinking in the saying is that, if you want a positive relationship, it's important to make that first contact a good one. If you are ever trying to prove that the old saying is nonsense, Herb Magee would be a good counter-argument. His first exposure to the Philadelphia University (formerly known as Philadelphia Textile) basketball program would have given you little reason to think that the man who has won more NCAA men's basketball games than any other coach would step onto the Rams campus in 1959 - and never leave.

Magee was an explosive scoring guard at West Catholic High School who lived and loved basketball. When the high school season was over, he played in summer rec leagues. On this particular occasion the summer prior to his senior year, he was playing for the Cherry Tree Inn. As he puts it, it was "a bunch of old guys and me."

In the best-of-three championship series, Magee's team would be matched up with the team from Philadelphia Textile.

"At that time, whether it was legal or not legal, Bucky Harris - the coach - had his whole team, including him, in the league."

Magee would have a big game, leading the Cherry Tree Inn to victory in Game #1 of the series.

"Next game - second play of the game - "I go in for a lay-up," Magee remembers. "I will never forget this. I got my legs cut out and as I look up wrapped around a pole - it's Bucky. He's the guy. I looked up and he was standing over me. That's something for a young kid."

You can argue the merits of a coach taking it to a high school player like that, but Magee says you can't argue the effectiveness.

"It worked because you start looking over your shoulder. So we lose that game and then the championship game we lose as well."

And that was how Herb Magee was introduced to Philadelphia University.

"Lets go ahead to my senior year in high school. The following January, I'm walking in to go play Monsignor Bonner and I see this guy that cut my legs out. The game is over. I have a decent game. My coach Jack Devine comes down and says, 'There's a coach here that wants to talk to you.' Turns out it's Bucky Harris. So I go, ok. I'm kind of not paying attention because this guy almost killed me."

However, Harris was taking a multi-prong approach to landing Magee.

"He starts recruiting me through my uncle. We were orphaned at a very early age and an uncle, who was a Catholic priest, raised me. He took in the four boys in the family. So Bucky finds this out and starts to recruit my uncle and my uncle fell in love with Bucky."

Magee did draw some interest from bigger schools like Richmond and St. Bonaventure. But when the money was on the table, he says it came down to what his uncle said.

"He had our best interests at heart and he said you should go play for that guy Bucky Harris. So I did. And that's how I got here. The rest is history. I've been here my whole life."

Magee would get the chance to unleash his offensive skills on

Ram opponents, skills that he had honed, not just at West Catholic, but also in those summer rec leagues.

"That was our act then. Every recreation center in the city had a league and we were in just about all of them."

These summer leagues provided not just an opportunity to play basketball, but also to pile up some pretty cool memories.

"There were no cell phones at the time so what we would do is, one of our guys who wouldn't play would go by the pay phone at the rec center. Another guy would be by the pay phone at another rec center. Then they would call each other, 'what's go-

Herb Magee arrived at Philadelphia Textile (now Philadelphia University) in 1959 - and never left.

ing on?' 'Well we're up twenty'. 'Alright, we're sending a car for Herb and Bobby Gormley, (who was a guy who played at West Catholic) to bring them up here because we're down ten.' So the other guy would say, 'Use your time outs, we'll be there in twenty minutes.' So we would get out of the car and run in and try to save the game."

But it wasn't just amateurs that laced them up around the city.

"I remember one night going down and watching Earl Monroe get 50 for one team and Bill Bradley score in the 40's for the other team. These are two guys that probably played in the previous NBA All-Star Game," remembers longtime NBA coach and Magee's West Catholic teammate, Jim Lynam. "To play against a Walt Hazzard and Wali Jones at a swim club would be no big deal. I tell players over the years that Herb would hold his own. Those guys would have trouble guarding him, because he is one of the best shooters I've ever seen."

Magee would step right in for the Rams as a freshman in 1959 and Coach Harris gave him the green light.

"I started every game from when the season started and he recruited me to score, and he made sure that I got shots. There wasn't a shot that I wasn't allowed to take and he would encourage me to shoot all the time."

The Rams now play in a beautiful new state-of-the-art facility, the Gallagher Center, right on campus. When Magee arrived at Textile in 1959, the team had a bit more of a "nomadic" quality to it.

"We had to go every day my freshman year down to 5th and Allegheny to Mann Recreation Center for our practices and games. The following year they opened up what is now Harris Gym and we were in there for some 40 years maybe."

Magee would lead the Rams to great heights during his four years on campus and score an awful lot of points doing it, many of those points coming on his patented jumper.

"I had good spring. I could jump and I had the ability to shoot it off the dribble. I could go one or two dribbles going either way and get in the air quickly and be able to shoot it. It would be the same with me shooting it if I was standing still, which I worked on. I had the ability to shoot it standing still and the ability to shoot it off the bounce. And once you get to that point, you are going to be a tough person to guard. I would stop and shoot off the break rather than go in for a lay-up and things like that. And when you have the green light, it's amazing what that does for your confidence, and I learned that from Bucky."

"At an early age, like a freshman in high school, maybe even 8th grade, he had a focus on practicing shooting," Lynam remembers. "And he understood shooting as a very young guy. Now how he did it, I have no idea. I used to ask him as we got older, did he have any serious instruction? But he's the type of person who can teach himself. Like he taught himself tennis, he taught himself golf and to me I was always amazed – obviously of his ability – but his understanding at such an early age of the mechanics of shooting."

Magee says his shooting touch was no accident.

"I would practice or play basketball literally every single day. In the winter I was here with the team practicing. In the summer I had a job, but I would also practice at night, play at night. Weekends, I was in the gym all the time. I would shoot literally like 500 shots a day. I just would keep working, working, working until I got to the point where I felt like I could make every shot I took. And once you get to that point, that's how you become successful."

ABoth he and his team were successful, with his college playing career being crowned by a special senior season. The Rams would go to the NCAA Tournament in 1963 and win the Eastern Regional Championship. They would get as far as the National Quarterfinals before losing to Oglethorpe from Georgia.

"We were 5-10, 5-11, 6-2, 6-2, 6-2 (in height). They come out and they were like 6-3, 6-5, 6-8, 6-9 and 6-10 (in height). But they were also a team that held the ball. The whole game, every time I touched it, all five guys on that team were hollering my name, 'Magee, Magee, Magee.' I'm looking around the first couple of times like what is going on around here. I guess their idea was to try and stop me. We ended up losing. One of our players unfortunately called a 6th timeout and the technical foul cost us the game."

That would be the end of Magee's days as a college player. He would finish his career with 2,235 points – without a three-point line – which was good for an average of 24.3 over 92 games and is still third on the Rams all-time list. He shot an even 50 percent from the field, and 86 percent from the line. His career would draw the interest of the NBA, and the Boston Celtics selected him with the 62nd pick of the 1963 draft.

"It was exciting because I never expected it. It turns out their scout saw me play in Evansville against Oglethorpe."

However, Magee had broken fingers on his shooting hands playing summer ball.

"Now for me to go up there and make the team without being able to shoot the ball was impossible – A. B - this was their back court – Bob Cousy, Bill Sharman, Sam Jones, K.C. Jones and John Havlicek. So to say I would make the team was maybe a long shot. But the fact that I couldn't go without the use of my right hand, it was a waste of time. If I hadn't been injured, I would have gone up just to meet those guys. Meet Red Auerbach? Could have been at Red Auerbach's camp? I mean it's unbelievable."

This was also 1963, well before the time of million dollar signing bonuses. The decision to skip the Celtic camp also made financial sense, according to Magee.

"Let's say when I started working here (Philadelphia University) I was paid $5,000. If I had made the Celtics - maybe $5,000, that's what they were making. Good friend of mine was (the late) Paul Arazin, and Paul and I used to sit and talk about the NBA. He's one of the greatest players of all-time. When the Warriors left (Philadelphia) and went to San Francisco, he got a job with IBM because he could not afford to go to San Francisco and play pro ball. That's why he ended up playing in the Eastern League. Because he could not afford to take his family to San Francisco."

Magee would stay at Philadelphia University.

"I was hired to work for Rohm and Haas. I worked with them during the summer in the mailroom. They were going to hire me because my brother worked for them too. So I go to Bucky right before graduation, and said, 'I got this job but I don't really think I'm cut out to be a 9 to 5 guy' because I used to watch the clock the entire time when I was working during the summer. It used to drive me crazy."

Harris asked if Magee might have an interest in coaching.

"I said, 'Could I?' He said, 'Let me talk to Dr. Hayward.' Now Dr. Bertrand Hayward was the president here and someone asked me once about the influential people in your life. It was my uncle, Bucky Harris and Dr. Hayward. Dr. Hayward was a great man. He is the reason this university was here and he is the reason why this university got started. And he hired me."

Magee would wear a lot of hats in his new gig.

"They invented a job for me – cross country coach, teaching phys-ed classes, JV coach and assistant varsity coach for basketball. A year later, tennis coach. Ten to fifteen years after that, golf coach, intramural volleyball director. It was like what else can he do. But how many times do you get the chance to go and get a job at the school you just graduated from and also stay involved in the sport. It was huge for me. I couldn't wait to come to work everyday."

Magee would spend four years working as an assistant for the Rams, the first two for Harris before he retired, then a year with Jack McKinney who came over after serving as an assistant at St. Joe's.

"I learned an amazing amount of basketball just being Jack's assistant. I learned under Bucky, but it really grew when I worked with Jack for a year."

McKinney would leave after a year to replace Jack Ramsey as head coach back on Hawk Hill. Harris would then unretire and return to his post with the Rams, Magee still on his staff.

"Halfway through the year," he says, 'I made a mistake - I shouldn't have done this and you're going to be the coach.' Whatever he said happened, he said you'll be the coach next year."

Magee would take over the program in 1967, at the age of 25.

"When I first got the job, I got a book, a little pamphlet by Bobby Knight about playing defense. I used that as my bible. It was a caricature of a devil in an army uniform snorting and it was called *Let's Play Defense*. We still do the drills I learned from that book.

Then he put another one out called *Let's Get a Good Shot*. It cost like two dollars and I still have both of them."

Magee would win right away. In fact he still remembers that first win vividly.

"We beat Maryland State; it's now Maryland-Eastern Shore, a Division I school. They were one of the better teams around and we got them on their home court. I had a guy on my team named John Osbourne and he gets on the bus and he says, 'Coach, I've got a present for you' and he had the ball. I said, 'Where did you get this?' He says, 'I stole it.' So, years later, when we won 500 games, he is at the game at Dowling College, so he goes – guess what, I did it again. So, years later, I got an award and John was at the luncheon. I said, 'John stole the ball at my first win and he stole it at my 500th win to record the only two steals of his career.'"

One of the key players on the first Magee teams would be John Pierantozzi, a 6-4 forward out of St. Thomas More High School in West Philadelphia. Pierantozzi was actually recruited by Coach McKinney, but he knew about Magee.

"The first time I saw Herb was at Rose Playground at 75th and Lansdowne Avenue. I was working the scoreboard at a league they had there. It was one of those old time scoreboards where you had to kind of spin the numbers around. Herbie's team was playing against Earl Monroe's team and I literally could not keep up with how quickly they were scoring that night."

As it turned out, Pierantozzi would play for Magee's JV team as a freshman and then his first three varsity teams after he took over for Coach Harris.

"That's when I discovered that all the stuff that I knew about Magee - being a great shooter, a very good ball-handler, a guy who never, ever played any defense, a guy who never had an assist, a guy who never had a rebound - had all of a sudden become this defensive maniac, I don't know how else to put it. It was one of the biggest disappointments in my life because I'm thinking, 'Oh my God, here we go. We're going to play for Herb Magee and we're all going to end up scoring 20-25 points a game – it's going to be a lot of fun.' Little did I know that Herb started studying Bobby Knight's coaching manual and started to focus his coaching purely on defense first - rebounding, positioning, all of those things, and then ball control and controlled offense."

Magee's focus would prove right on the money, as his first two teams went 41-11 and advanced to the NCAA Tournament. Then came the 1969-70 season.

"We lose to Villanova – the next year they are in the Final Four, Final Game. We lose to them at Villanova Field House. Had them down 9 in the first half, should have won the game actually. We kicked it at the end. We then beat Drexel pretty good. We then go down and play Mt. St. Mary's and we had the game won and we kick it away and lose in double overtime. We're coming back on the bus and I'm like 1-2, but I know we're pretty good. I'm talking to John (Pierantozzi) and (Ram player) Carlton Poole and they say, 'Coach, we're going to win the rest of them, don't worry about it.'"

And so they did. The Rams went on a tear; they would run the table on their way to qualifying for the NCAA Tournament for the third straight year. And they didn't just win. They bludgeoned opponents. Their average margin of victory was over 24 points a game.

"It just was a blended team and we went through the season without injuries. They were a great basketball team," Magee says. "If you asked me was this the best team you ever had, I would have to say yes. They were just great players and they played together – they were cohesive. John was a great captain; he was a true leader. The players actually feared him more than they feared me, and he would dictate what we would do. He was great."

"We were on one of those rolls where we absolutely expected to win every game and win every game by a lot," Pierantozzi remembers.

"We won five games (in the tournament) and we won by 27, 18,

48, 16 and 11. I know I can tell you the exact scores of all five games," Magee says.

The final score of that final game came was 76-65, as the Rams defeated Tennessee State for the College Division National Championship. Back then, the NCAA wasn't broken down into Divisions I, II and III. It was simply University Division and College Division. The national title did breed a little cockiness in the young head coach.

"I made this statement and I hope I didn't say it to too many people. When it was over someone said, 'Way to go, you won the National Championship!' And I go, 'It wasn't that hard - we'll probably do it a lot.' That was 38-39 years ago and then you realize how hard it is because it's a one and done situation. I expected to win but then I saw how hard it was as my career progressed. It's a difficult thing to do - to be successful all the time - especially the big games, conference games, regional championships and then the goal every year is to compete for the National Championship."

During that National Championship season, Magee would welcome a young high school coach by the name of Dick DeLaney to watch one of his practices. DeLaney and Magee would begin to forge a friendship, with DeLaney having Magee up to speak at basketball camps he was helping to run in the Poconos.

"Many times in the summertime in the Poconos, we had (former Villanova coach) Rollie Massimino, Jim Lynam and Herb - those three guys would come up and I got a chance as a young coach to go out with the three of them and we'd talk basketball at night," DeLaney remembers fondly. "We'd talk about situations and draw plays on napkins in the bars having a couple of beers and Herb was just a great technician of the game, a great teacher of the game. That's what impressed me the most the first time I saw him and was able to see him in action. His attention to detail and his grasp of the x's and o's of the game was tremendous. And then along with that, the other things about coaching, your player/coach relationships, the organization, that type of thing and I was just very impressed with how he ran his show."

DeLaney would eventually join Magee's staff as an assistant in the mid-70s, spending more than a decade at Philadelphia University before taking over his own program at West Chester. There he would set the school record for career coaching wins before stepping down in 2008. In 2009, he returned to Philadelphia University to once again serve as an assistant to Magee.

"I think that I learned the game of basketball from Herb," DeLaney says. "I thought that maybe I knew a little bit of it, but I learned the game of basketball and I also learned about priorities about how you become a coach. There's a difference between running a collection of players and a program. That's what he has done there is run a program the right way. Kids graduate. You have relationships with kids. You go to their weddings. If someone passes away in the family, you go to the funeral. You run a program. When I left him in 1987 to do my own thing, that's what I took with me and was fortunate enough to continue that on."

As you can imagine, Magee's success at such an early age did lead to attention from other schools, wondering what it would take to pry him away from his alma mater.

"I actually interviewed at a couple of schools just for the heck of it," Magee remembers. "People always say, 'If you've been that successful, why didn't you leave?' This, as it turns out, is where I belong. I know that. And I've known it for a couple of years. I had schools that called me to interview for jobs —couple schools called me and offered me jobs. But they were out of the area and I didn't want to leave the area. I enjoy this area, this is my home, my family, my friends and my brothers. This is where I decided I was going to stay."

And Magee has no regrets about setting up shop with the Rams.

"I made the right move. I've talked with a lot of my friends over the years that have had different jobs in different places and they say,

'I'm jealous of you for staying where you stayed'. Because coaching is coaching."

While that 1969-70 season would prove to be the only National Championship of Magee's career, at least so far, it by no means was the end of his success. His program was mentioned among the national elite, and those wins kept piling up. Twenty-win seasons, NCAA Tournament bids and lofty slots in the national rankings are the norm for Philadelphia University basketball with Herb Magee at the helm. And to me, watching Magee's teams play, one of the most amazing things about his success is that he does it by rarely substituting. It is not unusual at all for Magee to have 3, maybe 4, or even all 5 players play all 40 minutes.

"I always wanted to coach someone as if I'm coaching myself," Magee says. "Now what did I want to do when I played? Let me play and I will do good things. Give me a chance, let me stay in the game — don't be pulling me in and out. First of all, I'll be in shape, don't worry about that. Secondly, if you take me out you throw off my rhythm. So I always have done that."

Magee says this philosophy has garnered some attention.

"The old expression was always 'you better have great lungs or a big ass to play for Herb Magee' because you're going to do one or the other."

"He has the other kids as part of the program and they know they are integral parts of the program, but their time will have to come," DeLaney says. "He just doesn't really care about substituting a lot unless he has to. What he'll do is he will just get a confidence level with a certain number of guys and goes with it. The way the game has changed with the speed and all the physicalness - it's a unique thing to find and it works for him. It's not going to work for everybody, but it works for him."

Another thing you can be sure of with Magee's team is they will be well-schooled in the fundamentals of shooting the basketball. Early in his coaching career, Magee spoke at a basketball camp. He was asked what he wanted to focus on during his talk.

"I said, 'I'm a good shooter. Let me talk about shooting.'"

And with that, another aspect of Magee's career was born.

"I've never lectured at a camp or clinic or anyplace without talking about shooting. So if someone says, Herb Magee's on the staff, they don't have to put down what I'm going to talk about. Everybody knows I'm talking shooting."

"There's a difference because not only can he shoot it with the best of them, but he has an ability (to teach shooting)," Lynam says. "I have seen a lot of great shooters. I have not seen a lot of great teachers of shooting. I've seen a lot of great coaches. I've not seen a lot of great coaches who can teach shooting. I can coach, I can't teach shooting."

Magee would quickly become the go-to guy for young players who wanted to learn the art of the shot. However, soon it wasn't just amateurs he was helping. Jack McKinney had moved on to the NBA. He was now coaching the Indiana Pacers and his team needed help shooting the basketball. He reached out to Magee.

"Jack calls me on the phone – 'Do you think you could help our team? I know you can really shoot because I worked with our players when he was coaching here,'" Magee remembers. "So I went out and stayed with Jack for a week and went to his training camp and during the day, double sessions. I'd have George McGinnis, Clark Kellogg and work with them individually on foul shooting. They really enjoyed it. Jack might have been the first coach to have somebody in just to work on shooting. So they went from last in the league in foul shooting to like 2nd or 3rd. So Jack then gets the job with the Kansas City (now Sacramento) Kings and I went out and worked with those players."

This success led to spreading the word that he was able to get through to NBA guys.

"Matty Goukas (then Sixers coach) calls me and says, 'Can you come over to one of our practices – I want you to meet this guy Charles Barkley.' So I go over and meet Charles and I'm just working for a couple of minutes because he's not interested. I consider Charles a friend of mine, but his attention span is about 30 seconds and he's not interested. I just got him to do a couple of little things and it really improved his foul shooting. So word gets around."

Lynam, who has spent decades coaching in the NBA, says Magee's success with the top caliber players is no accident.

"All you have to do is get your guy in the gym with him. One thing about the NBA player is they know who knows what they are talking about and who is 'Mr. Buzzword.' They know the difference."

While he schooled players of all kinds in the finer aspects of shooting, Magee's teams also continued to win. One class in the 90's went their entire four-year career without losing a home game – the Rams winning 80 straight at home from 1990-1995. One of the players to come through the program around this time was guard Jesse Balcer. An Abington Friends product, Balcer walked on to the Ram basketball team after he says Coach Magee called him out of the blue to encourage him to do just that. As expected, Balcer didn't play a whole heck of a lot, and after his sophomore year he was thinking of giving up basketball and concentrating his energy on his other athletic passion - baseball.

"Even though I didn't play a lot of minutes, Coach talked me into staying because he felt like I had a big impact with the team. It's hard to find somebody that isn't playing all the time that will pick everyone up when things are going bad and find the positive out of the negative and kind of rally guys around even though you aren't on the floor at the time. I think he saw that in me and he really talked me into staying and sticking around because he needed me. And that meant a lot to me so I stuck around."

Balcer would eventually be named a team captain as a senior. Upon graduation he would help enhance another aspect of Magee's legacy, following in his footsteps and becoming a basketball coach.

"(Playing for Magee) had a major influence because I think learning from him gave me so much confidence," Balcer says. "I kind of feel like I know more than other people because I played for him and I learned from the best. The main influence was playing and learning from him and watching the way he did things - gave me the confidence to know that I can do it. And know that I kind of have the inside track on a lot of things and the way things work. His teaching style on offense, the way everything falls into place and knowing the way he taught it."

Balcer would actually serve as a Magee assistant for three years before getting the head job at Chestnut Hill College. He is one of numerous former assistants and players who have moved on to take over their own program.

Through the years, Magee would pile up more and more victories. 600. Then 700. Win #800 would come in December of 2005. Then on February 1st, 2007, Magee's Rams would take the court at the Gallagher Center on campus with history in their sights. With a victory over 0-20 Wilmington College, Magee would become the all-time winningest coach in the history of Division II basketball.

"That game goes overtime against a winless team. Winless. We had beaten them earlier in the year by 30 - they did show up with two new guys who could play. But I do think our players reacted to the capacity crowd, everybody with microphones and television cameras and all that kind of stuff."

It wasn't pretty, but in overtime the Rams would eventually pull away and give Magee his 829th career win by a final score of 65-60 - the win total was now one more than legendary coach Clarence "Big House" Gaines and the most ever in Division II history.

"I remember congratulating the other coach, saying 'good game'

JASON MINICK

The 2009-2010 season was Herb Magee's 43rd as Head Coach at Philadelphia University.

and I turn around and I'm mobbed with a million microphones and so on and so forth," Magee says. "My granddaughters, my daughters, my wife – well my wife stays in the stands — but my granddaughters know the cameras are on so they come out and get a little shot in the paper."

The 2009-2010 season represented a half-century of basketball for Magee at Philadelphia University. On February 13th, 2010, once again in front of a packed house at the Gallagher Center, Magee picked up his 900th career victory. The Rams held off Bloomfield College 81-77.

"We made the plays when we needed to make them, especially defensively. And any time you do that you're going to be successful," Magee said afterwards.

With the win, Magee became just the third coach in NCAA history to hit the 900-win plateau, joining Bobby Knight and Don Meyer of Northern State out in South Dakota. However, Magee and Knight are the only two coaches to collect all their wins in NCAA games as Meyer had a number of wins in NAIA competition carry over. Magee passed Knight on February 23rd, 2010, when he won his 903rd game in front of a capacity crowd at the Gallagher Center, his Rams beating Goldey-Beacom College 76-65. When it comes to men's coaches who have won all their games in NCAA play - Herb Magee's name is now alone at the top of the list.

Needless to say, through the years, Magee has seen the basketball landscape change and the kids that play for him change as well.

"The kids are a little bit different, but if you luck out and you do your homework recruiting, you get the right one. They're good kids. They are different. They are a little bit more 'what's in it for me?'"

Magee remembers one conversation with a potential recruit that highlighted this point.

"An expression a couple years ago was touches, you're in the game and players want to 'touch' the ball. So I told the kid, last year we shot 46%, that means we missed 54 percent of our shots. You want to touch something? Go touch those, because 54 percent of our shots are laying someplace 'up there'. Go touch them and then you'll be my hero. He didn't really get it, but you think I'm going to have you touch the ball just to have you touch it? That's not the way we play."

Magee has found plenty of kids that do play the right way, however, and he still enjoys the wins as much now as he did when he started.

MATT LEON

Herb Magee addresses a packed house at the Gallagher Center after his 900th career coaching victory.

"Absolutely, and the most fun you have is - it's been a close game, there's still time on the clock and it's been a war. But you have done some things, your team has done some things now you can see you're going to win and here's the clock going 30, 29 or 10, 9, 8 and you know you got it and that's the most fun you have as a coach, in my opinion. "

He loves sharing the big victories with those closest to him.

"For afternoon games - we go to my house with my brother and his wife and my children and my grandkids. We will have some people over, get some pizzas and a couple of beers. If the game is during the week I go home and just sit there with my wife and she'll go over the box score and stuff like that. She's a real fan. She's great. She loves it."

So what about retirement? Can he see a future that doesn't involve Ram basketball?

"Never enters into my mind until someone mentions the word. The only thoughts I have about this job are we have four seniors on this team (09-10). We must do a good job this year recruiting. Then we are worried about next game, practice. That's the only stuff that enters into my mind. But I do know this, when the time comes I will know. Because (right now) I don't even think about it."

The scoreboard tells the story of Herb Magee's 900th career coaching victory. His Rams beat Bloomfield on February 13th, 2010.

The 2007-2008 Ursinus Men's Basketball Team

"The further away we get from it, the more I realize how lucky we were and how special it is, not that many people can say they were a part of something like that."

– URSINUS CENTER MICHAEL SHEMA

I am convinced that the NCAA Basketball Tournament is the greatest thing going in sports. Nothing beats a deep run in March. While the Division I Tournament draws just about all of the nation's attention that time of year, the Division II and Division III Tourneys are just as exciting. They just don't get 1/100th of the media attention. The lack of cameras and microphones, however, does not lessen the magical quality of advancing to the Final Four. To prove this, look no further than Collegeville, Pennsylvania in March of 2008.

Usually when a team puts together a run to the Final Four, I find it follows along one of two story lines. The first is the "Cinderella." That really has become a very common term in today's sports jargon, but for those unfamiliar, I will explain. That's a school that has never been there before that really captures the imagination of its fans and the public. Then there is the "Coronation." That's where a really good team winds its way through the tournament, justifying its lofty

URSINUS ATHLETICS

Ursinus Coach Kevin Small celebrates a Trip to the Final Four

ranking in the process. What I think makes Ursinus' experience extra special is that it is the rare case where elements of both story lines come together.

The seeds for the 2007-2008 campaign for the Bears were really planted the season before. One of the hallmarks of Ursinus basketball since Kevin Small took over as coach in 2000 is that the Bears almost always play better basketball at the end of the season than they do at the beginning. That, however, was not the case at the end of the 2006-2007 campaign. Ursinus lost its last four, including a first round game to Haverford in the Centennial Conference playoffs. That was

Michael Shema's emergence was a big reason why Ursinus advanced to the Final Four.

a finish that was unacceptable to many, most notably Nick Shattuck. A La Salle High product out of Ardsley, PA, the 6-5 guard had developed into an elite talent at the Division III level and the unquestioned leader of the Bears.

"I think junior year, the troubles we had toward the end of the season really hit home with me and made me much more dedicated in the offseason to not letting that happen again senior year."

Having the reigning Centennial Conference Player of the Year focused on a mission is a great arrow for a coach to have in his quiver, but Small says there were other aspects of this team that pointed towards the upcoming season being different. One was an intriguing talent that Ursinus was going to have to lean on down low. Michael Shema was entering his senior year. His first three seasons had seen him start but one game, but Small was tweaking the Bears offense – experimenting with a four guard look that would take advantage of talents like Shattuck, and guards John Noonan, Remy Cousart and Matt Hilton. A look like that however would need a true big. And at 6-10, some 280 pounds… Shema was big.

"He saw the writing on the wall, like 'Wow I have an opportunity here to really create a special role for myself,'" Small remembers.

"I felt like Coach Small made it pretty clear to me from the beginning," Shema remembers, "clear that he trusted me and I was going to be given the opportunity to take responsibility and get more minutes and have the team rely on me."

Shema's story is a wonderful one and probably could get a chapter in this book all to itself. His parents were from Rwanda and by the time he arrived in the US for his senior year of high school, which he spent at a boarding school in West Chester, he already had lived in Switzerland, Ivory Coast and Belgium. It was in Ivory Coast that he first started to really give basketball a try at the tender age of 15.

"I didn't know anything about basketball. I was just trying because I was so tall."

He would learn the game quickly, and Coach Small saw enough in him to bring him to Collegeville, and eventually get him in a position to make a real contribution his senior year.

Small takes pride in playing all comers, peppering the Bears' non-conference schedule with some of the best Division III has to offer. The 2007-08 season was no exception, as Ursinus opened the campaign at the Rose City Classic at Drew University in Madison, NJ. In their first game, they would play perennial Division III power Williams. The Bears played well, but lost 88-73. However, Small saw a lot he could take from the season-opening effort.

"We played a really, really good game. We scored some points (73) and lost, which meant it was easier to go back and show film because that team was going to have the potential to score points. We could come back knowing we were eons away from the teeth of our league schedule and show film right away against a perennial top 20 team and say, 'What if we had defended this way instead of what we did?' They (Williams) were defending and we managed to put up (73) points. What if? And I think that helped us for sure."

The Bears would win their next six games after Williams, leading them to a trip to Immaculata on December 19th, the final game before Christmas. Immaculata was a program that had improved by leaps and bounds over the past few seasons, but to this day you can still sense the annoyance in Shattuck's voice when he thinks back to an 87-77 defeat.

"They were a good team, not to take anything away from them, but they were a team we should have beaten and we all knew that. I think coming back from Christmas break we realized that if we wanted to be this top tier team, we really had to devote our time and effort in practice and focus on the little things."

Small thinks the loss did indeed help focus his team as they rolled into the calendar year 2008.

"Losing to Immaculata did something to this team, there is no denying that. When we went to Daytona Beach, Florida a week, week and a half later at the (Land of Magic) Classic, we were clearly in a different place as a group."

At the tournament in Florida, the Bears would beat two good teams in RPI (Rensselaer Polytechnic Institute) and Middlebury, and then play at home for the first time in a month. That game against Trinity would prove to be a defining moment in a special season.

2007-2008 Ursinus Men's Basketball Team

URSINUS ATHLETICS

Nick Shattuck battled through injuries in the NCAA Tournament to lead the Bears to the Final Four.

"Trinity's a powerhouse," Small said. "And we beat them pretty soundly (69-56). We were up big at half and we were able to get guys into a rotation, the kind of thing that is unheard of against a team that good."

For assistant coach Brian McEvily, the Trinity win was a moment to really take stock of what was happening with this group.

"Trinity is a team we'd been playing for seven or eight years and we'd never beaten them. We were always giving Coach a load of crap because (Trinity coach) Stan Ogrodnick had his number and we just couldn't beat them. But Nick Shattuck kind of took it upon himself to make sure that before he graduated, Coach could say he got Trinity one time. We all looked at Trinity as a pretty mature and accomplished program. So to beat them - a good team, outside of our own conference, was a big deal."

The Bears would continue to build momentum. The win over Trinity left them at 9-2 and rolling. They would eventually steamroll the rest of their schedule, finishing undefeated in the conference.

They would take a 23-2 record into the Centennial playoffs, which they would host in Collegeville.

The plan for the season really had come together. Shattuck was on his way to being named conference player of the year again. John Noonan had become that critical second scoring option. Sophomore guard Matt Hilton also provided scoring punch and a great touch from the perimeter. Point guard Remy Cousart was a stabilizing force, while also leading the team in rebounds. And Shema thrived in his first year as a starter in the middle. His development gave the Bears that presence they so desperately needed down low at both ends of the court.

As for the conference tourney, first the Bears dismissed Dickinson 93-79. They would then play an excellent Gettysburg team for the title and the conference's automatic berth to the NCAA Tournament. Ursinus swept the two regular season match-ups from the Bullets, winning by a combined 55 points. The conference title game would prove to be much more difficult, but Shattuck would pour in 31 points to lead the Bears to an 85-78 win. Ursinus was heading to the NCAA Tournament.

"To beat a solid team like Gettysburg, three times in a row in one season is always tough to do. So we beat them, big sigh of relief," McEvily remembers. "Then we look at the NCAA Tournament. We were anxious about how we are going to be seeded."

I mentioned in the beginning how this Ursinus NCAA run would prove to be a wonderful blend of the expected and the unexpected. Let me expound. Under Small, the Bears had really emerged as a top tier Division III program. This would be his team's fourth appearance in the Tournament since he took over in 2000 and the third win over Gettysburg would improve him to 4-0 in Conference Championship games. So this is a program that knew lofty status. However, the Bears had yet to win in the NCAA Tournament under Small, losing the first game in all three previous appearances. Any kind of run would also have an excitement attached to it that you can really only experience your first time.

As a top seed, the Bears would host at least the first two rounds. The first opponent would be Baptist Bible College out of Clarks Summit, Pennsylvania on Friday night, March 7th. This was a match-up that heavily favored the Bears on paper, but given their disappointments in previous NCAA Tournaments, Small was taking nothing for granted. He remembers his preparation for the Defenders bordering on the compulsive.

"We were going to know everything they do. Now things might not go our way, but I and my coaches will do everything to prepare our guys. Now at the same time I knew deep down we were a one seed and they were a 16. And I knew what their talent level represented and that they were going to be playing on the road in our gym and I know what our gym is like in the postseason and I knew there were going to be 3,000 crazy people there. It (a loss) was not likely. But I remember being as prepared as I possibly could be."

Assistant coach McEvily says the match-up would give the team a chance to prove that they learned a valuable lesson from the regular season.

"The Immaculata game - that was a game where we learned, if we don't show up, if we don't play, if we don't prepare, we can lose. So you can't take an opponent lightly."

It was obvious from the outset that the Bears had learned that lesson and learned it well.

"We kind of shook their world for the first ten minutes," Small remembers with a smile. "They really even had a hard time getting the ball over half court and setting their offense up."

Ursinus scored the game's first 13 points and never looked back, eventually winning the game 94-76. However, early in the second half, the good feelings that a first-round win would provide were significantly tempered. Shattuck, who already had several thunderous dunks to his credit, stole a ball in the front court and was going in for yet another slam when he was fouled hard by a Baptist Bible player.

"I was taken down on the dunk and actually landed with all my weight on my right heel and bruised the heel pretty bad to the point where it was really painful to put any pressure on it at all."

Shattuck would come out of the game, which was unusual in itself.

"He's a tough kid," McEvily says. "Nick's gotten up before, he's limped around. He's been ok."

The training staff worked on the heel and wrapped it in a way designed to take the pressure off. Baptist Bible, to its credit, did not go quietly and stayed just close enough that Shattuck returned to action a few minutes later.

"But because of that (the heel injury) there was a chance that, with it elevated, it could turn and that's exactly what happened," Shattuck remembers. "I ended up turning the ankle as well so my whole right foot was pretty much done at that point."

2007-2008 Ursinus Men's Basketball Team

The Bears were able to coast home against the Defenders and win that first NCAA Tournament game under Small, but with their second round match-up set less than 24 hours away, the coaching staff had its work cut out for it.

"The job became preparing for life with Nick and without Nick," Small remembers. "So your job became double the workload because you are going to have a scheme based on with him and without, and that was almost singularly our focus. As a staff, there was no wild celebration (after the Baptist Bible win), there was no exhale."

Literally hours before the game on Saturday, Shattuck was cleared to play, as it was determined that the damage that was done to his right foot couldn't get any worse. His injury really made life difficult because of the Bears' next opponent. Virginia Wesleyan had appeared in the National Championship game the previous two years, winning it all in 2006. Any kind of a break the Bears got with the first round draw of Baptist Bible was more than evened out by getting a team this seasoned in round #2. In the first half, it really looked like Ursinus was in over its head.

"They dominated us in the first half. They really wiped the floor pretty good with the Ursinus jersey," McEvily remembers.

The lead for Virginia Wesleyan was 17 at the break and the Bears were searching for answers. While Shattuck was playing, he clearly wasn't himself and in this game he eventually would sprain his left ankle as well, a result of trying to protect the other one too much. The Bears' best player was literally playing without a leg to stand on. But in a bizarre twist, Shattuck's physical shortcomings would really help lead the Bears to a remarkable comeback.

Defensively, Coach Small is a man-to-man guy at heart, but Ursinus needed to "hide" Shattuck because of his lack of mobility, so Small made a change.

"Only because of that (Nick's injury) we played a ton of match-up zone, which ended up being kryptonite to this poor Virginia Wesleyan team."

Offensively, Small also changed his philosophy on the fly.

"The second half of that game became 'we are going to give the ball to Mike Shema.' We are going to force these forwards who are incredibly athletic and mobile to defend a big guy the right way. Because they were cheating on everything and Mike Shema had this incredible second half."

"Yeah, I felt like I should take on more responsibility," Shema remembers. "I guess everyone on the team felt that way. We were all going to have to push harder to advance and to perform well. It was a very natural thing that happened."

In the opening moments of the second half, Wesleyan pushed its lead to 19 points, but then the Bears started their comeback. The zone was forcing missed jump shots and things were getting easier for the home team on offense, thanks in large part to Shema. The 6-10, relative newcomer to the game was enjoying his biggest moments in the biggest game of his career.

"Mike stepped up, man," McEvily remembers. "I mean he was a stud. He was hitting turnaround baby jump hooks that at 6-10 you just couldn't guard."

While Shema excelled, Small says it took all the Bears' firepower to complete the comeback.

"We had some really terrific individual performances late in that game, among them Nick. All five starters had a specific play to help us win that game. Remy had a big play and Matt Hilton hits a huge pull-up jumper in transition."

That shot by Hilton down the stretch was when Shema says he realized that they had the game won.

"I could tell they were falling apart. You could tell we were going to be able to pull this one out."

The Bears would advance to the Sweet 16 with a 70-64 win. Hilton led the way with 17 points, Shema added 16. Despite the injuries, Shattuck would gut out an 11-point performance while pulling down a team-high 9 rebounds.

"It was obviously really, really exciting for our fans. At that point you were really excited for them because they were just phenomenal. The student section en masse was just beside itself during that run in the second half," Small remembers. "Runs have a funny way of affecting everything. The opposing team was falling apart at the seams because they just can't believe that this match-up zone is doing to them what it's doing to them. The crowd is doubly loud, the officials are caught up in that comeback - a call that might not go our way ten minutes into the first half when everything was going to Wesleyan does go our way in the second, that 50-50 call. And I remember after the game, being so excited for our kids because they got the chance to keep playing."

Now the Bears would have the better part of a week to prepare for the Sweet 16 and to figure out where Shattuck was physically. But who would that next opponent be?

"I still remember standing on the court after the Virginia Wesleyan game. The emotions kind of run their course - it was a very emotional comeback," McEvily says. "It was a big win and we were all feeling pretty good about ourselves and when we came back up to the locker room and everybody wanted to know what was going on with our next opponent and so we heard the recounts. Buzzer-beater. Three-pointer to win the game. Incredible win. We were all kind of like, 'Aw man. We got Gettysburg again.'"

Yes, the team that Ursinus had spent the season stealing the proverbial lunch money from was back for more. It would be a Centennial showdown to go to the round of eight.

Despite the two bad ankles, Shattuck would be ready to go once the Sweet 16 rolled around. And while he was not the player that he had been during the regular season, you have to marvel at the way he seamlessly adjusted his game to his physical limitations.

"My role had shifted at that point. I knew that I wasn't capable of doing the things I had done for my whole career, in terms of offense. My focus was more on helping the team out defensively, re-bounding doing what I could from that standpoint, distributing the ball, trying to take attention away from other players to give them an opportunity."

Nick Shattuck and the rest of the Bears took the court on March 14th against Gettysburg. Once again, Ursinus would host and Collegeville was ready for the Sweet 16.

"We've beaten them three times," McEvily remembers thinking before the game. "They are the second ranked team in the region. How many times can you beat a good team like Gettysburg?"

The answer to that question is apparently four because the Bears rolled. John Noonan had 22 points and Shema was marvelous once again. He hit 9 of the 10 shots he took from the floor en route to a 21 point, 10 rebound night. Ursinus 79 Gettysburg 55.

Used mostly in that game to draw attention away from other players, Shattuck had just 10 points, but Coach Small says that was enough.

"Nick had a couple of plays where he actually did things on the court – not as a decoy but rather as Nick Shattuck –'Player of the Year.' That was enough to reinforce him being a decoy. He was good enough that they had to checkmate 'that' Nick Shattuck, which gave us the ability to knock their king over later in the game."

To put this dominance in perspective, that Gettysburg team was 24-1 against squads that did NOT have Ursinus across the front of their jerseys.

"When you play a team four times, inevitably there is a chess match that goes on with any of these games. We're no dummies. There is a lot of energy that goes into scouting and we had seen some fairly sizable changes to Gettysburg's strategies in the Centennial Conference Finals and some of them caught us off guard. And perhaps that's why that game was closer. But we had the benefit of seeing that and counter- punching. And the counter-punches worked."

The fourth victory over Gettysburg left the Bears one win away from the Final Four. The only thing standing in the way from a first class trip to Salem, Virginia? The United States Coast Guard Academy.

The true "Cinderella" of this tournament, Coast Guard had won a school record 24 games under veteran coach Pete Barry. But few people outside of New London, Connecticut (where the Academy is based) saw the Bears getting to this point.

"We knew nothing about Coast Guard Academy," Small says.

However, Small says they got a bit of a break when it became apparent that Coast Guard played a style that they could get their arms around with so little time (less than 24 hours) to prepare.

"In some ways, we benefited from United States Coast Guard Academy being a team that on some level, the way they played resembled Centennial Conference play. So we were able to use the scheme that we were most comfortable in playing to try and compete against them."

When you get matched up with a team that isn't supposed to be here, there is always the danger of taking them for granted, especially when a prize like the Final Four is waiting on the other side.

"I think actually Coach Small and the coaching staff did a very good job of keeping us focused on this game and this game only," Mike Shema remembers. "We were just focused on beating Coast Guard and playing our best game in an important moment."

Forty minutes would not be enough time to decide this game. The team headed to overtime tied at 69. Small says it was the type of game you want to decide a Final Four berth.

"It was fun, that's for sure. I remember Remy Cousart made some big plays down the stretch, made two free throws at money time in a wire game. He buries the front and back end of a one and one to get to overtime."

That came with seventeen seconds remaining in regulation. Coast Guard would miss a three for the win and they headed to overtime. The visiting squad would take a 71-70 lead in the opening moments of the extra session, but Ursinus would take control from there.

"(Cousart) has two turnaround fade away plays, these crazy basketball plays in overtime," Small says. "Matt Hilton made some big plays. John Noonan made some big plays."

Despite the two bad ankles, Shattuck would put up his best numbers since the opening round – going for 19 points and eight rebounds.

"Late in the game all the adrenaline was flowing. We had gotten a rebound and I was leaking out and with all that adrenaline and the crowd going nuts I went up for the dunk. My last two points at home came on that dunk. From that point on you heard the crowd start chanting 'Final Four.' That was a crazy atmosphere. I'll never forget that feeling."

"That moment after that game (82-76 win) was about as high a sense of just joy for the moment, because I was just so happy for our kids," Small remembers. "They were running around like crazy, the crowd rushed the court. It just this ebullient atmosphere, everyone celebrating and I just remember thinking, 'This is why you are a Division III basketball coach.' Now I know the celebration that goes on in Division I and the glitz and what that gives you in terms of money. But there is something so authentic about that moment in a Division III gym, where these kids are going to go off and be attorneys and doctors. This is just about true sport in that moment. And these kids are just crying tears of joy."

Once the celebrations subsided, it was time to focus on the task of preparing for the Final Four. The Bears' opponent would be Amherst, another national power out of Massachusetts. Aside from basketball, the pageantry of the Final Four - well Small says that was pretty cool.

"The NCAA does it right in terms of their postseason stuff. It was all that you would think a Division I Final Four would be. There were lots of bells and whistles and we're at a five-star hotel. It was just spectacular. Everything was beautiful and gift packages for every kid."

2007-2008 Ursinus Men's Basketball Team

There were also moments which reminded everyone they weren't in Collegeville anymore.

"When we got down there and got off the bus, there was a guy with a camera," McEvily remembers. "He was there to get a reaction and watch us unload our bus and get into our hotel. That was when you kind of went 'Whoa, what's going on here? This is a little different than just any other game.'"

But as daunting a task as getting to the national semifinals was with Shattuck beaten up physically, winning here would be even more difficult given the quality of the opponent and the deterioration of Shattuck's ankles physically.

"At no point did I want to show anything or say anything to anybody," Shattuck says. "But I could feel it personally, physically, that it was getting tougher and tougher each game with my ankles. They were getting worse and worse. I couldn't move during the week, in between the games. I didn't practice at all the last three weeks. I just sat down icing and rehab."

Shattuck would play against Amherst, but for the first time an opponent had the means and the time to game plan to specifically take advantage of his lack of mobility.

"They did a lot of screen to screener stuff," Small remembers. "They made Nick have to negotiate screens as a defender and made shots off of it. (On offense) we had parked Nick inside a lot because he didn't have the same explosion. So we allowed him to play with his back to the basket a little bit. Well, for the first time in weeks Nick wasn't double teamed in the post."

The Bears would be down 11 at the half. They would battle, but eventually the bigger and, more importantly, healthier Amherst team took control of the game in the second half. Despite 18 points from Noonan and a 13 point, 10 rebound night from Shema, the Bears' magical run ended with an 84-58 loss.

"They really shut down what we did best, our shooting from the outside, our fastbreak," Shattuck says. "They really scouted us well

URSINUS ATHLETICS

Ursinus went 29-4 during a magical 2007-2008 season.

and handled us with ease. Got to give them all the credit in the world for the way they played against us."

Now, in Division III they still have a consolation game where the two losers of the National Semifinal match-ups battle for 3rd place. Ursinus still had one game left; they would play Hope College out of Michigan. However, with the chance to win a National Championship now off the table, Small and his staff handled this game a bit differently.

"I knew that there were a lot of guys on our roster who hadn't played a big role on the court who deserved the opportunity in a Final Four. So we decided we would offer up opportunities for all of our guys to contribute and compete. And I think in that way we look back and it's something to feel really good about."

Nine different players played double-digit minutes in a 100-86 loss to Hope. One of them was not Nick Shattuck. His college career ended at the opening tip. The two teams had agreed to a ceremonial jump ball, allowing Shattuck to start the game and then immediately be subbed out so he could get the adoration his career so richly deserved.

"The entire student section stands en masse and starts chanting 'MVP' for Nick. So that was a neat moment."

"It meant a lot for Coach to let me do that," Shattuck says. "Go in there for the jump ball and go out on the court."

The season ended with that loss but the Bears held their heads high. Sure there was disappointment, but they were quite aware of what they had accomplished.

"Looking back on it, it was the best experience of my life. There is nothing that comes close to that run we had. It was the best three weeks of my life," Shattuck remembers. "My mom after every year goes through and finds all the newspaper clippings and all the online articles. She puts together a scrapbook for me. I was looking through it and you know, just thinking back on all the little things, you forget about the season. Just seeing everything that we did and all the amazing times that we had together. It was an amazing year."

Small says that year helped crystallize the lofty status of the Ursinus program for the public. But for him, it was simply a high point in what has been a wonderful journey at the head of the Bears' program.

"I have the best job in America. I get to work with kids every day that are inspiring to me. I get more out of it than they ever get from me. And I get paid to do it. That's hard to believe."

Marilyn Stephens is the only Temple women's basketball player to have her number retired.

Marilyn and Dominique Stephens

"My brother's a good recruiter.
He recruited me."

– MARILYN STEPHENS ON WHAT
BROUGHT HER TO CHEYNEY

As the men's and women's basketball coaches at Cheyney University, the fact that Dominique and Marilyn Stephens are brother and sister makes for a good story in its own right. However, when you talk to them and see how close the bond is between the two, the story crosses over from good, to special. That bond became apparent to me when I interviewed them together in the studio. Both outstanding players in their own right, I was curious who would win when they would battle each other on the playground growing up in Philadelphia's Nicetown-Tioga neighborhood.

"Not battle," Dominique Stephens quickly corrected me. "We always played together. We usually won a lot playing together."

That, I do not doubt.

During their childhood, faith and music were the main focuses for the six children in the Stephens family. Mom and Dad were separated, but both parents were very involved in their children's lives. Mom, Evelyn Stephens, juggled her job as a reading specialist at Grover Cleveland Elementary and her positions as the church pianist and children's choir director at Second Baptist Church in Nicetown with raising six children. Marilyn says their mother also made sure they were very active kids, helping plant the seeds for basketball success, but not necessarily in ways you would think.

"We were very athletic, thanks to my mom who always had us involved in riding bicycles and as a kid I would jump rope all the time, you know, not thinking that double-dutch would help my agility on the court," Marilyn remembers. "And my brothers would roller skate all the time, so that worked on muscle development and balance."

Mom says those active days were special with her young children.

"We would play basketball at the park, but we weren't into it like we were with our roller skating and our bike riding," Evelyn Stephens remembers. "We used to ride from the Cheltenham Mall all around City Hall and back to Nicetown. We used to go down the parkway, East River Drive, run up the Art Museum steps, and the bike route there. Mom in front, and all the little ones in back."

Basketball, in fact, did not really become a staple for Marilyn and Dominique until high school.

"We were both late bloomers," Marilyn says. "I didn't really start playing serious basketball until 10th grade. And Dominique was playing football, soccer and swimming so we got into basketball in high school. And we just focused on 'hey we like it' and just practiced hard to get better."

While basketball arrived on their scene relatively late for them, both had success in high school. Marilyn was a standout at Simon Gratz. Dominique played at Dobbins where he spent time on the court with such legendary Philadelphia high school talents as Doug Overton, Bo Kimble and the late Hank Gathers.

Mom says the two also excelled in the classroom.

"They both studied hard. They both were interested in school.

Marilyn Stephens took over as the women's basketball coach at Cheyney in 2008.

It's a wonderful thing. They loved learning. No running up and down the street acting silly. They loved learning."

Marilyn is four years older than Dominique, so she set off for college first, staying in Philadelphia to go to Temple where she dominated as a 6-1 power forward/center. In fact, any conversation of the city's best women's college basketball player has to have her in it. Her career on North Broad Street was so successful that she was Temple's first Women's Basketball Kodak All-American and to this day she is the only player to have her number retired (#33).

"I take it as an honor to have a number retired. Sometimes when people see me or they meet my children, they'll tell stories, 'Your mom played and she was great,' and all that stuff. To listen to it, it's like 'Wow, I didn't know they felt like that.' When you're playing you don't hear it. But as years go on, coaches I had met or coaches that my team (Cheyney) played against that were coaching when I played, they will tell me, 'Yeah, we used to try and box and one you or we used to try and do different things.' Just to hear it now is like 'Wow.'"

By the time she graduated in 1984, she was, and still is, first on Temple's all-time list in points (2,196), rebounds (1,519) and blocks (342), among several other stats. For her career, she averaged 18.8 points, 13.0 rebounds and 2.9 blocks per game. That was more than enough to earn her a spot in the Temple Hall of Fame.

Following graduation, Marilyn spent a couple of years as an assistant coach at Temple and then went overseas to put the uniform back on, playing for a year in Italy and Spain. It's a year she looks back on fondly, remembering playing in front of sell-out crowds. But she missed her family and was spending way too much money on long distance phone calls, so she returned to the states and to coaching, accepting an assistant's job at Florida International University.

As Marilyn's playing days ended, Dominique's college career began as he headed down to Division II North Carolina Central in Durham, North Carolina. While he didn't put up the jaw-dropping numbers his sister did, Dominique's team had phenomenal success, winning a Division II National Championship his junior year in 1989, in the midst of a three-year run that saw NCC go 87-12. During that National Championship season, the 6-5 swingman was named to the NCAA Elite Eight All-Tournament Team. That championship team is forever enshrined in the North Carolina Central Hall of Fame.

"Just the feeling of being at the highest point of winning at the level of the sport you are playing is amazing. It was an unbelievable situation."

Dominique would cap his career by putting up his best numbers as a senior for the Eagles. He would also go overseas for a year, playing in the Philippines. That time, however, was not quite as memorable as Marilyn's experience on foreign soil.

"It made me want to come back and get my bachelor's degree."

Dominique soon picked up the three credits he needed to get that degree and eventually (along with Marilyn) earn his Masters Degree. He would go on to spend some time in Lancaster, Pennsylvania, playing for the Storm of the Eastern Basketball League and working as a teacher with special needs children.

"That's a part of my life I enjoyed."

A new opportunity came about in 2003 when Dominique's old college teammate, Cleo Hill, Jr., was named the head coach at Cheyney and asked him to join his staff.

"His coming here was a big reason for me coming here. I have a lot of friends who played at Cheyney and graduated from Cheyney. That was another part because I knew the history of Cheyney, the love that those guys had for the university. I just thought it would be a perfect fit for me as an assistant."

Meanwhile, Marilyn was still in Florida. After her time at FIU, she got into teaching, eventually landing a job teaching Phys Ed at Coral Reef High School in Miami. She also spent several years as the head coach at Coral Reef, the BOYS head coach.

She says it was no big deal to her or her players that she was a woman coaching boys. But she would get the occasional parent asking, 'How can you coach my son?'

"Just like a female English teacher can teach him English, they are teachers. You don't take your child out of the class because he has a female teacher and put him in a male teacher's class. It's the same way with basketball. Skills are skills. The way I teach a right hand lay up is the same to a girl as it is to a guy."

Her players also had her back from day one. And they knew that she had game.

"One of my guards told someone who said, 'Aw, y'all got a female coach!' Well, she's got more clout than you, where have you played professional ball? She has more rep then you have. How many records did you break?'"

Marilyn soon stopped coaching because the long hours made life difficult as she was raising a family. Her oldest daughter, also named Marilyn, would follow in mom's footsteps with high grades and a love for music and eventually head to Florida Atlantic University on a track scholarship. While no longer coaching, she remained a very popular Phys Ed. teacher. Marilyn also spent countless hours working with disabled athletes and, in fact, was honored with the David Bercuson Award for Outstanding Coaching for Disabled Athletes.

While Marilyn had been down in Florida for nearly 20 years, her family back home in Philadelphia was never far from her heart. Constant phone calls and frequent visits helped bridge the distance, but Marilyn missed everyone and was looking to come home. But it had to be the right opportunity.

In 2008, Cleo Hill left Cheyney to take a position at Shaw University in North Carolina. And that opened the door for Dominique to get his first head coaching job, as he took over the Wolves on an interim basis. Then the women's job at Cheyney opened up when Darryl Brown left for a gig at Pepperdine. If only Dominique knew a

Dominique Stephens keeps a close eye on his Cheyney Wolves.

standout women's basketball player with ties to the Philadelphia area. Needless to say, little brother called big sister and let her know that Cheyney had an opening.

"We talked about it, prayed about it," Marilyn remembers. "I talked to my mom about it, my daughters - everybody was included in the decision making."

The idea that Marilyn could be coming home was news that mom was very happy to hear.

"I shouted a little bit. I was so happy!"

As you can guess, Marilyn got the job and basketball at Cheyney was now officially a family affair, and then some. Dominique was already coaching his son, Dominique Curry, on the men's team. And now Marilyn would get the opportunity to coach her sister Marian's daughter, Angel Stephens, on the women's team.

"I missed my niece being born and here I can catch up with all those years. And I missed her playing in high school, now here I can teach her in college. It was a big bonus in the decision making to come here."

But the opportunity to work with her little brother was without a doubt the driving force in this equation.

"Without him, I don't know if I would have been here. Truthfully. I mean I had a good situation in Miami."

Both coaches started their initial campaigns as head coaches at Cheyney in 2008, leaning on each other for support, at the same time impressing each other.

"The guys respect him and they listen to him. He has a passion. You have to have a passion for coaching because sometimes you might not see the reward right away, but it's the passion that keeps you going," Marilyn says. "He loves his job. When he gets up in the morning and he leaves late at night. And he's putting those long hours in and the dedication is outstanding. So I really admire him for that and I'm proud of him and how he really puts himself in his job."

"To see my sister practice at 5 in the morning and then to see her when I'm leaving at 11 at night, she definitely puts the time in. Very dedicated to the program," Dominique says. "I also like the way she is able to deal with so many mentalities and attitudes with the girls on the team. She deals with it very well. She is able to relate to all of them, no matter if they need to talk to her for a mother's opinion, coaching tactics or as a sister. She's able to relate to her girls very well."

Marilyn and Dominique Stephens

The Stephens' family ties aren't just limited to the court or the sidelines, as you'll often find family members watching the Wolves play basketball, especially Mom.

"Very thrilling. Very uplifting," Evelyn says. "It's wonderful because I think they are doing what they love and I am here to see this. It is the highest point. I just sit back and enjoy and praise the Almighty. That's what I do."

"She loves good sports," Marilyn says. "She loves when it's played at its best, when you are doing what you are supposed to do."

And, Marilyn adds, all six of the Stephens children strive to be the best, in large part because of the impact Evelyn, their mom, had on them.

"She always made us feel like we could do whatever we put our minds to."

While Dominique and Marilyn have excelled in sports, everyone in the family is quick to point out the wonderful careers that the rest of the children have had in other fields. Zack is a computer analyst, Marian drives an 18-wheeler for the post office, oldest sister Vivian is in real estate, and oldest brother Ray is a retired Septa bus driver. Zack and Ray are also musicians in their spare time.

Dominique's men had an outstanding 2008-09 season, going 18-9 and, soon after, Dominique was rewarded with the removal of the interim tag and given a three-year contract. Marilyn's women went 12-13, with those twelve wins representing the most for the program in 19 years.

So while Coach Stephens and Coach Stephens both enjoyed first-year success on the court, it was trumped simply by the opportunity for brother and sister to be side-by-side once again.

"I get to see her every day," Dominique says. "Growing up seeing her every day, its back. I'm back with my big sister."

Coach Mike McLaughlin keeps a close eye on his Holy Family squad.

Mike McLaughlin

*"I don't demand to win or lose.
I demand to have success and compete
every play and every day. And I think that
translates into success, which in this sport
translates into wins and losses."*

– MIKE MCLAUGHLIN ON HIS COACHING PHILOSOPHY

T he first time I researched Mike McLaughlin's head coaching record as I put together a story on his work at Holy Family, I admit I had to look twice. The winning percentage was so outrageous, there had to be a misprint. I mean, I didn't win 87% of my games when I played Madden Football on PlayStation and the computer was on the rookie skill level. But sure enough, the coach who arrived at the 400 win plateau faster then any coach in women's basketball history (at any level) had won 87% of his games at Division II Holy Family before getting hired at the University of Pennsylvania in April of 2009. Another remarkable aspect for McLaughlin is that he has put these stunningly good coaching numbers up almost immediately after a playing career during which he NEVER won a pro game, in some 550 tries.

A 5-9 point guard with a lethal touch from the outside, McLaughlin was a Northeast Philly kid who went to Father Judge High School. A broken leg his senior year took him off the recruiting radar for a lot of schools, but Holy Family showed interest and he would become a Tiger.

"It was a neighborhood school at the time. It was somewhere my dad wanted me to go because it was closer to home and it was somewhere he thought I could have success, both academically and athletically, and it was more kind of out of I didn't have a whole lot of options."

However, it would prove to be one of the best decisions McLaughlin would ever make.

"I was fortunate to walk into a situation when they were building a program so I was able to play right away. I flourished right away. I got bigger and stronger. Coach Dan Williams was my college coach there and he put us in a great situation."

McLaughlin would leave his mark on the Tiger record book. He is the school's fifth all-time career scorer and third all-time in assists. He is also the best three-point shooter the program has ever known — over his four seasons he would connect on 57.7% of his shots from behind the arc (161 of 279).

As his college days wound down, McLaughlin caught the eyes of a regional scout who wanted to bring him on board his pro team.

"He happened to see me play at a college game. He approached both my coach and my father my senior year. They were interested."

Soon after graduation, McLaughlin would become a member of the Washington Generals, the long time foils of the Harlem Globetrotters.

"Mike came to our attention through some people in the Philadelphia area who were familiar with Holy Family basketball," says John Ferrari, who has served as the Generals GM for some three decades. "In looking not only at his stats (at Holy Family), but also his mental make up, he was a perfect fit to be a Washington General."

"I later found out that they liked the way I conducted myself on and off the court. I didn't know that at the time," McLaughlin says. "So that's important for me as I move forward in coaching now. To let everyone know that at some point, someone's watching you. But that was a good life lesson for me and you know I was given that opportunity once I completed school. It was the best thing that ever happened to me."

But that doesn't mean leaving home was easy, as McLaughlin was involved in a relationship with the woman who would eventually become his wife. He had met Ginny when they were in grade school and the two started dating in high school.

"It was tough just because I knew the amount of travel that was involved," Ginny remembers, "but he is two years older, so I still had two years of college left so I guess that part made it easier and actually helped me concentrate on school better."

MIKE MCLAUGHLIN

Mike McLaughlin having some fun before his Washington Generals play the Globetrotters in Orlando.

McLaughlin's first experience with the Generals, I imagine, is pretty much what your first day at your first job out of school was like.

"I didn't go to training camp because it was the middle of the season, it was July. I only know these guys from what I saw on TV. We meet at LaGuardia (airport). Now all these Globetrotters that I remember seeing on TV in the commercials are now in this same room with us, having a press conference for us ALL to go to Russia, a place at the time they hadn't been to in 30 years and I'm a little bit in awe of what's going on, let alone going overseas for the first time. We finally arrive in Moscow. I remember it took me at least 24 hours to get there and I'm overlooking Red Square."

This would only be the first of many extraordinary experiences across the globe that McLaughlin experienced as a member of the Generals, experiences that he says really helped shape him as a person.

"We went to Armenia and Armenia had an earthquake in 1988

MIKE MCLAUGHLIN

McLaughlin (shooting) and the Generals make an appearance on ABC's Wide World of Sports on Paradise Island in the Bahamas in 1989.

and we were there in '89. Houses were destroyed and I was like, 'Where are we going to play this basketball game? Who has the money to come to this game?' We are staying in a pretty nice hotel and I look out the window and people are living in tents. And wouldn't you know the next day we go over to play the game, 4-5 thousand people in a sold out arena screaming our names and it was just like 'Wow, this is real.' Who would have ever thought a kid from the Northeast would be in Armenia playing basketball with the Globetrotters. It was surreal. There's people living in tents less than 100 yards from my hotel that don't have a penny. At the time Russia had the ruble; they didn't have any money as it was, their money had no value. And here I'm getting 90 rubles a day; these people are making 90 a year. I'm giving out rubles to these people like I'm a philanthropist. It was kind of like the best feeling of my life, that I was in a position where I was giving people money. And as small as it was, I was able to give them something. I was able to give them some of my sneakers that I had five pairs of. I was able to give them a T-shirt. I was able to give them a pair of jeans that they didn't have."

"It changed me to this day. It made me mature really quick. I had a perspective on something that I was not ready for. At the time, I was blown away with what I saw. We all see TV, we all see dilapidated houses, we all see third world countries, and we see kids walking around with just pants on. You see it on TV all the time. I saw it 100 yards from the hotel and then went 3 miles down the road and played in a basketball game where these people were at the game. It made me say 'Wow. This is what the Globetrotters are.'"

Although McLaughlin was travelling the world and having the experiences of a lifetime, his heart was still in Northeast Philadelphia, and he and Ginny would keep in contact whenever possible, although it was often hard to match schedules when you're halfway across the world.

"A lot of times it would end up being the middle of the night for me when he would call," Ginny remembers. "Between the time differences and when he could get an open line, it would be 3 or 4 o'clock in the morning and the phone would ring and I would know who it was. That was way before cell phones and cheap calling plans so we had some really expensive phone bills. There were a lot of handwritten letters that he still has. And I would get a lot of postcards from him, wherever he was in the world."

So as far as basketball, how does the whole Globetrotter/General dynamic work? Is it real? Is it fake? Are the Globetrotters really that good? Can the Generals possibly be that bad?

"It was scripted in certain areas. They used to call them 'reems' when they went into that magic circle. That was all scripted and we would play the good guy there and allow them to do what they had to do and play the acting role if we had to. That was all scripted. The basketball portions were just basketball. Whatever happened, happened. It enabled us to be able to play, but we had to understand what we were doing, what our role was, and when we went into these 'reems' we just played the straight people and let them perform."

So McLaughlin played some 550 games as a General, but never once was he able to walk off the floor with a win.

"We came very close several times," McLaughlin remembers.

As McLaughlin explains it, the "reems" where the Globetrotters would go into their patented weave or magic circle were the key. Many times when things would get tight or uncomfortable for the Globetrotters, they would call for the scripted "reem" to help them reestablish control of the game.

"So when it got to be a two-point game, (they) would call it and we would have to let them go and they would lay it up. And they would lay it up. Now they are up three or four."

It was a fascinating dynamic between the Globetrotters and Generals, and one that McLaughlin says could have its frustrating moments.

"When you played a live ball and you go in for a shot and they knock you into the stands because we are playing real and then a play later you have to let him dunk it, now that's a tough thing to do. And when you do it every day and you live on the road with them every day and we all live with each other and the competitive side kicks in, it's easier said then done."

"We knew if we beat them it would (make news) around the country. That was our big thing, but we also were reminded all the time what our role was and our role wasn't to lose. Our role was to allow them to do the show. For someone outside the scope of what I'm talking about it's very unique, 'so did you let them win?' No, we didn't let them win. We had to give them so many and to make it up on the other end is nearly impossible."

McLaughlin would spend some three years travelling the world, playing basketball and entertaining thousands. Soon though, the desire to settle down and start a family with Ginny brought an end to his pro basketball career. But it would also lead to the start of his coaching life.

"It actually worked out in a weird way. I was done playing with the Globetrotters and I was working out one day at Holy Family and the women's coach at the time (Kathy Killian) asked me if I wanted to be a part of her staff as an assistant."

After a short stint as an assistant, McLaughlin took over the reins of the program when Killian left.

"I was in the position where I enjoyed what I did. I thought I was doing a pretty good job teaching. I enjoyed the recruiting and she resigned. So at that point I had a tie to the program, I had a tie to some of the recruits. I built some relationships with the players and I went on and was very fortunate to become a head coach at a very young age (28)."

The fact that he entered the coaching ranks came as no surprise to McLaughlin's former general manager, John Ferrari.

"Mike has a passion for it. Mike has a passion for people, so I knew he was going to get involved in some way, shape or form with something to do with people. So when he returned to Holy Family back in basketball, I knew that it was perfect. He gravitated to the woman's game. Mike's an immensely fair man and he's an immensely goal oriented man - but in a very positive way. There's no beating someone down to get what he wants. The winners in all that Mike McLaughlin does are his players."

He would start his first season in 1995, his Tigers competing at the NAIA level and in the Central Athletic Collegiate Conference. That first campaign saw Holy Family go 25-8, an incredible first season. Heck, an incredible season under any circumstances. But to put McLaughlin's coaching career in perspective, those 8 losses would be the most he would experience in any of his 14 seasons at Holy Family.

"It (that first year) didn't come easy but it was probably my best year of coaching. It was fun; I didn't know what to expect. Every day was new. It was a challenge but it was fun at the same time. I was just really fortunate. We had some success that year and we just built from there."

To say the least. The next three seasons would see McLaughlin's Tigers win 28, 32 and 29 games respectively. In the process, his teams qualified for the NAIA Tournament every year and reached the 100 win plateau during the 1998-99 season, doing so in just 118 games. It was around that fourth year at the helm of the program that he says he started to realize he was having more success than your average coach.

"That's the first time I really even thought about it. We were just coaching every day, enjoying what we were doing, but that was the first time I really thought about how quick this was being done. We didn't coach that way; we didn't treat the players that way. We didn't make it a demand to win. It was just one of those things. It just happened."

And it kept happening. One of the players that McLaughlin brought in to create and maintain this level of excellence was point guard Bernadette Laukaitis. Her older sister Tricia, also a point guard, had played at Holy Family and as she wound down her high school career at St. Hubert High School on the corner of Cottman & Torresdale in 1996, McLaughlin convinced her to come to Northeast Philadelphia to run the point there as well.

"I wasn't even sure if I was going to play basketball because of my height. I was small. I didn't think I could play at the college level," Laukaitis remembers. "He had an unbelievable talk with me when I was a senior in high school and told me that he wanted me in the program and I can do anything. He really made me feel very comfortable and let me know that I could do it at that level."

Laukaitis would go on to play the point for McLaughlin through the late 90's before graduating in 2000. A three-year captain, she is still in the school's top ten all-time in steals and assists.

"He just really got the best out of everybody that came through his program. And the one thing that I really respected about him is that he knew how to coach women. He knew how to relate to us very well and he found that perfect medium where he knew how to get us where we needed to be, but also had that understanding factor."

Laukaitis says it also didn't take long for her to see why McLaughlin was piling up wins on the court at an outrageous pace.

"He didn't just say 'Okay we are running this offense and that's the only thing we are going to do.' He was able to adjust according to the different personnel that he had. Not many coaches do that. Many coaches stick to what they do. I think that's what really separates him in regards to the x's and o's. I think he really makes sure that he puts in the correct things that will get the most out of his players, not just do the same thing every time."

Laukaitis would go on to join McLaughlin's staff at Holy Family after she graduated, one of several former players over the years he has brought back to work with him on the bench. Her work there eventually got her a gig running her own program at Cabrini College. She took full advantage of the opportunity, winning 23 games and taking her team to the NCAA Tournament in her one season at the helm. She only spent one season because, in 2009, she resigned to team back up with McLaughlin when he was hired at Penn.

"Leaving Cabrini, that put a big butterfly in my stomach. I remember thinking, 'How can I leave this? This is what I worked so hard for.' But at the same time I could not imagine doing something I have dreamed of doing - coaching at the Division I level at an unbelievable place with anyone else but Mike. If some other random person had asked me to come coach with them, I don't think I would have left."

McLaughlin would hit the 200-win mark during a 30-2 2001-2002 campaign, needing just an amazing 235 games. Another reason that McLaughlin was having so much success — defense. His teams would constantly be among the nation's toughest to score on when it came to points per game and field goal percentage. To play defense like that, you have to buy in to what a coach is telling you. And McLaughlin says a lot of that goes to bringing the right type of people into his program.

"I always ask the question, 'How important is it to you to play basketball here at Holy Family and now Penn? How important is it to you to not only get a great education, but to invest yourself in this basketball program? How important is it for you to play basketball here and represent this program and keep this tradition building?' I think if you ask that simple question and then read the answer, I think you might right away know how bad that player wants to be at your school and compete. They all come in as individuals and we have to build the team."

That team concept is another trademark of McLaughlin's teams and one that other coaches have taken notice of. As Philadelphia University head coach Tom Shirley, whose team is usually battling Holy Family for CACC supremacy, has told me on more than one occasion when talking about McLaughlin's Tigers, "Whatever 'it' is. They have 'it.'"

In 2003, Holy Family transitioned up from NAIA to NCAA Division II in basketball. That's a big jump and one that can cause a program to have to take a step back as they adjust to a higher level of competition. And the Tigers did take a step back. All the way from 30-2 in 2002-03 to 28-4 in 2003-04. That season also saw the Tigers qualify for the NCAA Tournament, something they would do every year under McLaughlin.

"There wasn't even a transition (from NAIA to NCAA); we made the tournament right away. I was confident that things were in place, the players were in place. The program was healthy."

The wins and the postseason opportunities would continue. Not only were McLaughlin's Tigers winning the CACC on an almost regular basis and qualifying for the NCAA Tournament annually, they were continuing to push the bar higher. Not just being satisfied with making the tournament, they would eventually start to do damage once there.

"It was so hard at times to be able to find the words every day to keep raising the bar, because here we have consistently won 25 games and now we have a new group of freshmen coming in. How do you develop them but not right away put them in a position where they had to win. That's a hard thing in this sport when you have to win, and that's why I think I fell into not talking about the wins and losses and just let the kids compete and play and develop and challenge them. Everyone wants to raise the bar; we just had to find ways to continue to raise the bar without putting pressure on the team to win."

After first round exits in their first two NCAA Tournament appearances, the Tigers would advance to the regional semi-finals to cap both the 2005-06 and 2006-07 seasons. That 2005-06 season would also see McLaughlin win his 300th game, becoming the fastest coach in women's basketball history to hit that milestone (349 games).

The 2007-08 season was McLaughlin's most successful in terms of results, which is obviously saying something. Holy Family would finish the regular season undefeated, roll through the CACC Tournament and earn a #1 seed in the NCAA Tournament. And for the first time they would win their way into the regional final before losing to a very good Franklin Pierce (college, not the president) team.

The next season would see the Tigers have more success. During a 26-6 campaign, McLaughlin would win his 400th career game as a head coach at Holy Family, becoming the fastest coach in the history of women's basketball to do so, needing just 459 games. The Tigers also went 18-0 in the CACC, the fourth straight year they would go undefeated in the conference. This season would end in the second round of the NCAA Tournament with a loss to Stonehill College out of Massachusetts. That would prove to be the last game McLaughlin would coach at his alma mater.

He was hired to replace Pat Knapp as the head coach at the University of Pennsylvania in April of 2009. McLaughlin had become synonymous with success and Holy Family basketball, making any decision to leave an incredibly difficult one. But he says the opportunity at Penn was a dream come true.

"Just perfect for me. Coaching in this great city, being a part of Penn and Big 5 basketball is something I have always dreamed about."

And the opportunity to call the storied Palestra your home court didn't hurt the job description either.

"It's amazing. The first time I went over there, I remembered back when I was kid, coming over and watching all the Big 5 games and sitting there with my parents. And now being able to say that's your home court, it's thrilling. Sometimes it's a little bit beyond words. I couldn't ask for a better situation."

His final tally at Holy Family: 407 wins, 61 losses. During his 14 seasons at the helm of the Tigers, he was named the CACC Coach of the Year, following 13 of them. His teams won ten CACC Championships and he says those are wins that really stand out.

"Every time we were able to win a championship and be able to step aside and let the players cut down the nets. I think those are the times that I've sat back and that's when I was most proud of what we did. It's more of a moment. I can probably visualize all 10 championships and where we were, what facility we were in and watching the team celebrate. I think that's the pinnacle of a coach. All that time, all that effort, all that talk about putting yourself in a position to win a championship and actually watch the kids that compete for you every day do it."

It's nowhere near over, but Mike McLaughlin's basketball career has already truly been amazing. Not many people can say they've literally traveled to the ends of the earth AND been mentioned amongst the best of the best doing something they love.

"I'm a basketball person and I think that's why I went into

coaching. My parents sacrificed so much for me; they drove me everywhere possible to be a player. We had a house down the shore; my dad would literally drive me to the city for a summer league game and drive back afterwards. That type of commitment was given to me and I feel I used it to hone my best ability. It gave me a chance to go to college. It gave me a chance to get here. My parents started it and I can finish it doing what I'm doing now."

So what about the irony of a man who never won a game as a professional player, turning around and doing almost nothing but winning as a coach?

"It is interesting," Ginny McLaughlin says. "He had to make up for all those losses I guess."

Philadelphia University Women's Basketball Coach Tom Shirley works the sidelines.

Tom Shirley

"He would teach you just so much more than basketball. He would teach you how you should be on and off the court and there are things that I do to this day which are things that he taught me."

- DARLENE HILDEBRAND,
FORMER STANDOUT GUARD FOR SHIRLEY

om Shirley's career as one of the winningest women's college basketball coaches not just in Philadelphia, but around the country, has always been a bit overshadowed. During his time at Division II Philadelphia University, his teams have consistently won twenty games, but the headlines in his conference always seem to be grabbed by someone else. First, by dominant St. Rose teams when the Rams played in the New York Collegiate Athletic Conference. Then when the move was made to the Central Atlantic Collegiate Conference, the Rams would always run into the buzzsaw that was Mike McLaughlin and Holy Family. Even on campus, the Rams men's team is coached by . . . what's his name again? Magee . . . yeah, Herb Magee. You know, the all-time winningest coach in Division II history. So it's always easy to overlook Shirley, despite a career win total which is approaching 600. However, my informal research has determined that there is one category where he has no peer. Most coaching wins by a former Ford Auto Company executive. Go ahead. Google it.

Shirley grew up a block away from Roxborough High School in Philadelphia, but went to Plymouth-Whitemarsh High School after his family moved at the end of 7th grade. From there, he attended Allentown College (now De Sales University), graduating in 1976. He played basketball growing up and through college, but wasn't really a head turner.

"I played in grade school where I peaked," Shirley says. "I went to high school where I was a decent sub. I went to college where I didn't play. And now I'm in the beer leagues on Monday night where I kill it."

So unlike most successful coaches, Shirley did not jump into the athletics fray after graduating college.

"I took my economics degree where my father told me I should go, which was the business world," Shirley remembers. "He got me a job at Ford Motor Company, the mother company, and in the mother company I was basically a zone manager (based in Pennsauken, NJ). I did that during a time when pickup trucks were really, really hot and Pintos were blowing up. So dealers would want to buy all of my trucks and none of my Pintos. My bartering skills were honed at Ford Motor Company."

However, after about five years of pushing those Pintos, Shirley realized that he needed a change.

"I was dating my soon to be wife and in April of 1981, I said to her, 'I can't do this for the rest of my life.' I was making $41,000 a year with a company car. I had just gotten promoted and was going to get a second company car and decided I wanted to go into sports. So I wrote letters and said I'll be the equipment manager. I'll be whatever. I'll wash jockstraps."

As luck would have it, there was an opening at his alma mater for an Athletic Director. Shirley says the President there, Father Daniel Gambet, had decided to hire someone with a business background and teach them athletics, after some controversy with the previous AD.

"He offered me a whopping $17,000. I traded in my T-Top Mustang for a used Escort, heard my father drop the f-bomb on me asking my mother if she dropped me on my head when I was young and didn't tell him, and got the blessing of my soon to be wife and went to Allentown."

In addition to getting the Athletic Director's gig, he says the president also offered him the women's basketball job.

"I said, 'Down the road I'd like to look at men's basketball' and he said, 'What's your experience?' Well, I coach in the Plymouth Junior ABA and I coach the Ravens. And he said to me, 'THE Ravens?' And I thought he was being serious because we were in first place at the time. It was just a little 10-year old boy's basketball team, but that was my claim to success. Hey, we were in first place. 8-foot baskets."

So Shirley reluctantly handed over the reigns of the Ravens and focused on the women's team at Allentown.

"That first year was really challenging because I had no concept of sets, no concept of running a practice. I'm 26, coaching 22-year-olds. Jack Branca, who used to coach Prep football back in the day, his daughter Mary Ellen was on the team and he came up to me one night and said, 'I see what you are trying to do and I think you are doing good things but you can't make chicken salad out of chicken sh*t. You gotta get players.' So the whole idea of recruiting, I guess I never really thought about it. I guess I thought in the beginning, I could take tomatoes and make a chocolate cake, because the Ravens were so good. So I went home and said to my wife, 'This whole recruiting thing I have to figure it out.'"

Shirley decided to start the recruiting process as close to home as possible.

"So I lived in Conshohocken. I went up to Archbishop Kennedy High School. Karen Kozniewski was the star player at Kennedy; everybody wanted Karen Kozniewski," Shirley remembers. "Bob Koch was the coach at Kennedy. Bob Koch is an Allentown graduate.

So I go over and my first ever coaching contact is 'I'm interested in Karen Kozniewski. 'Yeah, you and a 100 other people.' So I sit down with my wife. The game goes on. She says, 'You don't want Kozniewski – I don't? 'No, you want Nancy Irwin'. So I went to Bob and said, 'I changed my mind, I want to talk to Nancy Irwin.' So he brought her over, I proceeded to do my due diligence, got her on campus and she finally enrolled and she was the first piece of the pie. She was the first kid I ever recruited."

Shirley would continue to build the foundation.

"The next year I went over to Bishop Kenrick, which was the next closest school to my house and recruited Lynn Butler. She was the first mega-star, probably still in my top five players of all-time, and those two just made it happen."

"He had come to a basketball game to see somebody else from the visiting team and noticed me," Lynn Tubman (formally Butler) remembers. "He said he noticed my shooting in warm-ups and was interested from there and made contact. At the time Allentown College was NAIA, going into NCAA Div III, so I think probably the recruiting rules were a little different, because I did receive a lot of phone calls. I did receive a lot of letters and he basically let me know he wanted to have me be a cornerstone of a very young program at Allentown College."

Tubman says Shirley made an impression on her right away.

"Even during recruiting I went up to a game to watch Allentown, and he was animated on the bench. I had people in the stands ask me, 'Do you think you can play for someone like that?' I had a high school coach that was animated too and a yeller and expecting a lot, so that never deterred me. Then as a freshman making a couple of mistakes, being late to practice, laughing during the practice, I learned VERY quickly how serious he was and I responded to that. It motivated me to work harder and play harder."

Shirley would add two more key pieces during the mid-80s in Karen Povish and Tina Costello. Those four would form a nucleus that would raise the bar at Allentown, with the team becoming an elite squad and all four players rewriting the record book. Tubman is still the school's all-time leading scorer and rebounder. Costello is tops in assists. Shirley says Costello, a point guard, really had an effect on how he looked at the game.

"When I saw Costello practicing for me for the first time, I realized everything runs through your point guard. If you have the greatest chocolate and the greatest batter, but you don't have the person that can stir it, it's not going to work. Since then, I would say, if anything, I'm really partial and picky about my point guards."

Shirley's Allentown teams would become an elite NAIA team and then, in 1989, advance to the Sweet 16 of the NCAA Division III Tournament.

"I think if I stayed, the next year we would have won a National Championship. We were really good and really loaded."

But that would prove to be Shirley's final year at Allentown, as a position at Philadelphia Textile opened up.

"It was advertised as a 65/35 job of coaching, thinking I could be the Assistant AD – which is what I came in as - until 2 and then be the basketball coach. Whereas, at Allentown I was kind of the whole show without a lot of staff."

Shirley would make the move to then Philadelphia Textile, now Philadelphia University. He would be the women's coach, joining a basketball program which featured the legendary Herb Magee running the men's team.

"I remember my first conversation with Ted Taylor, the athletic director at the time. I asked him, 'How does the practice schedule work?' He said, 'Work it out with Herb.' So the first conversation I ever had with Herb, I asked how does the practice schedule work. He says, 'I've got good news. You have 22 hours a day to pick from but I go 4:30 to 6:30 [pm] everyday.' I go into Ted Taylor and say, 'Have you ever heard of Title IX?' He says, 'Yeah, but Herb goes from 4:30 to 6:30 everyday.' So that was that."

Shirley would pick another practice time and also develop a strong rapport with Magee - the pair becoming one of the most successful men and women's coaching tandems in the country.

"He's very gracious about his success and very complimentary about our success," Shirley says. "The kids get along, we promote that. He's not an us vs. them type of coach."

Shirley's first two years at his new home would be relatively non-descript. However, much like at Allentown, Shirley was building the foundation for success and that included bringing on Paul Stadelberger as an assistant coach.

Right around the time that Shirley took the gig with the Rams, Stadelberger was working in education and between coaching jobs. As he was looking at different opportunities, he got word of an opening on Shirley's staff. Stadelberger was a coaching veteran; he had worked with men's teams for six years at Haverford College. After the possibility of a job on the women's staff at Princeton fell through, Stadelberger focused on the opportunity with Shirley.

"I called Tom and said I was free and could come out and talk, but I really don't know anything about women's basketball. He said, 'That's okay' and I go out and watch the first practice at Textile. At the end, Tom comes up to me and said, "What do you think?' I said, 'Well, I told you before I don't know anything about women's basketball but you need some help.' And he said, 'Well you're hired.' And that's pretty much how it happened."

Stadelberger would spend 20 years as a member of Shirley's staff until leaving in 2009 to take over his own program at the University of the Sciences in Philadelphia.

"He has great passion for basketball, great passion for the kids and is very genuine and sincere," Stadelberger says. "You always know where you stand with Tom and there are no ifs, ands or buts about that. And he never made it seem like I was an underling; he always made it seem like I was a peer of his."

The two coaches' long history together led to Stadelberger almost being able to read Shirley's mind when it came to what he wanted to do in a game.

"Before Tom is calling a timeout I got everything ready to go on the sideline for a timeout. Like the last five years, if I felt like we needed to make a change on the floor I put a player in. I know one time like three years ago, it was a really tight game and there was this kid who gets in the game and she'd been in for about three minutes and finally he (Shirley) turns and looks at the bench and says, 'When did she go in?' I said, 'She's been in for like three minutes.' 'Well who put her in?' I said, 'I put her in.' He was like 'Oh, ok.' Right after he said that, he turns around and she makes a three point play and comes down and gets a defensive rebound. So it was like 'Ok, guess that worked out.'"

While Shirley found a trusted assistant, he still needed players. Once again it came down to recruiting.

"Tammy Greene came in and Tammy Greene was the Lynn Butler of Textile," Shirley says.

Greene was a star guard at Shirley's alma mater, Plymouth-Whitemarsh, and a Division I prospect, but she had fallen off the radar. The principal at Plymouth-Whitemarsh at the time, Pat Campbell, had been his homeroom teacher, and asked Shirley to take on a sort of mentoring role for Greene, the idea being that other schools would see her doing all the right things and then once again be interested in recruiting her. And it worked. Soon American University and George Washington started calling. Shirley was about to step away from the process, when he says Greene's grandmother stepped in.

"Her grandmother comes down to a meeting and when we're all said and done she says, 'Tammy Greene, you are going with that man.' Her grandmother just kind of put the hammer down," Shirley says. "She was the only four year starter we ever had."

Greene would be more than just a four-year starter, as she ended her career as the all-time leading scorer in Ram history and was the 1994 Division II Player of the Year. Shirley says she also brought toughness and swagger to the team and the program and cites two classic examples.

"Tammy Greene goes out to the center circle at the beginning of her sophomore year and bumps into Dawn Ellison from Mercy College, who was the returning NYCAC MVP," Shirley recalls. "Tammy says, 'Are you Dawn Ellison?' 'Yes I am.' 'You the MVP?' 'Yes I am.' 'I'll be taking that.' She was MVP her sophomore year, MVP her junior year, and MVP her senior year."

"Then her senior year we are playing St. Rose at home, and the coach of St. Rose walks in and says, 'It's BS that Tammy Greene has been player of the week six weeks in a row.' I say, 'I don't pick it, what do you want me to tell you?' I go to the locker room and say, 'Oh by the way Tammy, the coach from St. Rose thinks it's BS you've been player of the week six weeks in a row.'"

Shirley's squad would put together a great game, salting it away with time to spare.

"With one minute and ten seconds left we are up about 14 and I take Tammy out. She then goes out of her way to go all around the gym, walk past the St. Rose coach, shake his hand and whisper in his ear. After she comes down I ask what she said, and she said, 'I congratulated him on a well-played game.' So once the game's over, I shake the coach's hand and ask what she said. He says, 'She wanted to know if 38 points was enough," which is what she had that day.

Greene would be joined for much of her career by another gifted guard named Darlene Hildebrand, and Shirley would call them the best backcourt he's ever had.

"He was a great motivator," remembers Hildebrand. "He would tell you specifically when you did something right and compliment you, and when you did something wrong he would also get on you for it. He knew how to push the right buttons for each player; he was that good at it. Plain and simple, he was just a great motivator."

Greene and Hildebrand would help elevate the program in the early to mid-90s and start the tradition of winning and consistency. Consistency allows you to reach some lofty career win totals, and Shirley says he did start to notice that he was having more success than the average coach and that the win totals were piling up.

"I got very conscious of them when they started lumping me with Herb. I've seen 500, 600, 700, 800 and 900 with Herb and then they would say 500 (for Magee) and 'oh by the way' 250 (for Shirley), and they made a really big deal of it when we hit 1300 together, which was my 500 and his 800. And then they started comparing us to other programs, so I think PR kind of created that a little bit for us."

Talk to the people that he's worked with and you learn it's no accident he's had the success he's had.

"He relies on the players' abilities and skills, and he is able to read what they can do and then he uses that to his advantage," Stadelberger says. "He has a feel for how the game is going and knows what is needed out there at a particular time."

"The one thing I always say is he's very intelligent, he's very quick and he'll see things before a lot of other people and I do think that that's a strength," Tubman says. "You need to be able to see things quickly and adapt to them quickly and he does that extremely well. Defensively, he has so many different defenses that he will throw at an opponent at any time and I think that always allowed us to stay in the game."

"He knew every player's strength, he knew how to get them to use their strength," Hildebrand says. "He would work on your weaknesses, he just knew the game. If our inside game was hot, he would have plays for that. If you were hot, he would have plays for that. If you were having a bad game, he would try to get you in the game by calling a play just for you. Anyone can know the x's and o's if you study it, but he knew how to put it in play."

JASON MINICK

Tom Shirley and his Lady Rams are perennial contenders in the Central Atlantic Collegiate Conference

Win #500 for Shirley would come on January 5th, 2006 against Felician and it was a victory that circumstance did not allow to come easily, but made it a little extra special.

"Alicia Ferguson, our stud center, goes down 30 seconds into the game," Shirley remembers. "Well we were really thin on the bench so who do we have to put in, none other than Kristen Shirley, my daughter, who rarely played and wound up playing 17 minutes."

The game would be tight and history being on the line raised the intensity level even more.

"It was a back and forth game and with about 3 minutes to go, I remember taking a time out. I asked Jim Munn, my assistant, how many timeouts we had, how many they had, how many fulls, how many 30s and who should we foul if we have to foul. He tips down his Ben Franklin glasses and says, 'What am I f**king Rainman?' As serious as I tried to stay, he broke the ice a little bit with that; it did kind of calm me down. We made fouls down the stretch and won the game (90-81)."

Shirley is fourth among active Division II coaches in career victories. Aside from the basketball success, he's also built a legacy of helping his former basketball players and coaches on the court and beyond, teaching them lessons and providing examples they have taken from him to create their own success.

"I think he has a sense of trying to help people in every aspect of what they do on and off the court. If a kid messed up on the court, it didn't matter if they needed something after the game, he was there to help them," Stadelberger says. "If there was a kid that walked in the athletic office and wasn't even a basketball player or even an athlete that needed something, he went out of his way to help them. Those qualities of always being around to help people and wanting to help people and giving of himself. That's what Tom has always tried to do for everybody he's ever met and worked with."

"I would say to this day he is still a mentor," says Tubman, now the Athletic Director at Chestnut Hill College. "I am still on the phone with him frequently just getting his opinion and support on my career and family. Pretty much throughout my career he's been a guide and support for me. Even if I have a pretty good idea of the direction I want to go with something, I just run it by him and make sure I'm not missing anything or just for a pep talk when something is not an easy decision."

Safe to say that Shirley thinks he made the right choice leaving the auto world for the basketball court.

"The game itself is what I enjoy the most, the competition. The thing I love about coaching basketball is, if I was a car salesman and tried to sell a car, it may take me six months to get a result. It takes us 40 basketball minutes or 90 clock minutes to figure out – a winner and a loser. And no ties. And I like that. I love that competition. I think that's kind of cool."

Villanova Women's Basketball

"I needed the buzzer to go off
to make it real."

– KATIE DAVIS ON SNAPPING CONNECTICUT'S
70-GAME WINNING STREAK

Villanova Women's Basketball Coach, Harry Perretta, was on the team bus headed to the Louis Brown Athletic Center in Piscataway, NJ on March 11th, 2003, just hours before his team was to play Connecticut in the Big East Tournament Championship game, when his cell phone rang. It was the mother of the greatest player to ever put on a Villanova uniform, Shelly Pennefather. Pennefather is still the school's all-time leading scorer with 2,408 points and, at one time in the early 90s, while in Japan, was the highest paid women's basketball player in the world. But since 1991, she has heeded a higher calling, living in Virginia as a cloistered nun in the Poor Clare Monastery and taking the name Sister Rose Marie of the Queen of Angels. Her mother had called Perretta to talk to him about a story CBS wanted to do about Shelly becoming a nun.

"She asked me what I was doing at the moment and I said, 'Well, we are on the bus ready to go over and get our butt kicked by UConn,'" Perretta remembers. "She said, 'Why do you think you're going to get your butt kicked?' I said, 'Well, they've only won 70 games in a row and beat us by 20 the first time they played us.'"

Pennefather, however, was optimistic.

Villanova's win not only snapped Connecticut's 70-game winning streak, but it also won them the Big East title in 2003.

"She said, 'Well maybe things will be different this time. I'll call the monastery and ask Sister Rose Marie to pray for you guys.'"

But could divine intervention even stop Connecticut? One of, if not the premier program in Division I women's college basketball and the defending National Champions, the Huskies' 70-game winning streak wasn't so much a streak as it was a pillaging. Rarely were they threatened and this game, despite Villanova being ranked 18th in the country and bringing a 24-5 record into it, appeared to be little more than a speed bump as they rolled to another conference and national title. Led by future WNBA superstar Diana Taurasi, the Huskies had beaten Seton Hall by 23 and then Virginia Tech by 17 in the tournament to get to this point.

The Wildcats had advanced to the finals by outlasting Notre Dame and Miami the two days prior. They had played Connecticut once already during the regular season, back in January up in Storrs, and as Perretta said, lost by twenty. And in 2002, the Huskies had eliminated the Wildcats from the Big East Tournament with an 83-39 dismantling in the semifinals. The Wildcats were never competitive in that one, falling behind 19-0 to start the game. So the recent history did not bode well for the Wildcats heading in. But Coach Perretta had seen some signs in that 20 point loss during the regular season that led him to believe that maybe, just maybe, his squad had a little bit more than just a puncher's chance.

"There was a stretch in the second half where we were down 11 and we had gotten three wide open threes in a row and missed them. When the game was over, I said to Joe Mullaney, my associate coach, I said, 'You know on a really great night if they don't play well, I think we could win.'"

However, many of Perretta's players didn't really share his guarded optimism.

"We knew, obviously, that UConn was #1 and undefeated, so we were more just thrilled to be in the game, not really thinking that we really had a chance to win it," remembers Katie Davis, a senior forward on that team. "I can honestly say I don't think any of us thought we had a chance to beat them."

"I really didn't think that we had a chance to win," then senior guard Trish Juhline says, "which I was really cool with. I was just really excited that we had gotten to that point."

But being huge underdogs in a game like that left the Wildcats feeling loose. And that can make a talented team very dangerous.

"We had nothing to lose," Courtney Mix-Davis, a junior forward in 2003 remembers. "We were just going to play. We didn't have a streak going. We weren't even expecting to be there. So we just played."

Juhline remembers the pregame warm-ups, where Connecticut seemed to be brimming with all the confidence you would expect a 70-game-winning streak to provide.

"They were super confident. They were joking around and chest bumping and just doing things that were really irritating to an opponent. I remember me and Katie sitting there and neither of us said anything but it was just kind of like the roll of the eyes look, like 'they are so annoying' type of thing."

Coach Perretta says he made sure he pointed out to his team before the game the one advantage they truly had over the Huskies. Experience.

"They (UConn) were a young team; they had Taurasi but they had a lot of other players that were young. I said to them, the pressure of the winning streak will come to bear on them because the game that we are playing this night is a bigger game. So the bigger the game, the more pressure I think that would go onto them, there is no pressure on us."

As far as X's and O's, Perretta says they planned to do what they always did when they faced a more talented, more athletic team. Slow it down.

"Our goal was to keep the score low, keep the possessions to a minimum and just try to stay in the game. That was the goal, just try to stay in the game for as long as we could."

In the first half, the Wildcats more than stayed in the game. They dictated the pace and controlled the tempo. Utilizing virtually the entire shot clock possession after possession, the Wildcats slowed the game down to a crawl. And unlike the game in the previous year's Big East Tournament where the Huskies raced out to that 19-0 lead, it was Villanova that led throughout and took a 20-17 lead into the locker room.

"You could tell, even in the first half, that they were getting frustrated with each other, yelling at each other, doing things that we had never seen because we were always losing," Juhline remembers.

"I think they were frustrated because Trish was just making ridiculous shots," Mix-Davis remembers. "We would just make shots. And they don't really like playing our style I guess you would say. We would just walk the ball up and not shoot it until the last second. Maybe just a little frustrated."

The three-point lead was nice, but Perretta says the bigger key after twenty minutes was the fact that the game was indeed being played exactly like the Wildcats needed it to be played.

"Having the lead helped because it was a psychological thing, but keeping the score low was the biggest thing."

The Wildcat players knew that the chances that the Huskies would go away quietly were non-existent.

"UConn was notorious for coming out in the second half and just blowing people away, so we just wanted to keep playing our game," Davis remembers. "We were very, very excited that we had made it a game. We were thrilled. But we were realistic. We knew that that wasn't the game; the game wasn't over and there was still a whole half for them to get their rhythm back."

The second half continued to be played at Villanova's deliberate pace, but with the score tied at 25, UConn finally found their sea legs and went on an 11-2 run to take a nine-point lead at 36-27.

"When they started scoring their points it was kind of like 'Ok here they go - this is where they take over and take the game,'" Davis says.

Perretta had seen this movie before.

"It was exactly like the game that was up at UConn where we were down 11 with like ten to go."

However, this movie apparently had the bonus alternate ending. Instead of missing the open shots that in January had allowed the Huskies to put it in cruise control, on this night the Wildcats hit the open looks. Senior Nicole Druckenmiller buried a pair of threes, Mix-Davis hit a lay-up and converted a three-point play and just like that the Wildcats had regained the lead at 38-36 with 4:33 to play.

"At that point, you could see that we had gained back our confidence and they were a little rattled," Perretta says. "Because uncharacteristic of them, I think they turned the ball over two or three times in a row."

Juhline remembers that even when the Huskies took that nine-point lead, her squad just kept playing their game. She also remembers one huddle during a time-out when UConn was on their run where Perretta had scolded some players for passing up open shots - a no-no for the coach.

"That's always Harry's big thing, especially against a team like that; if you have a shot and don't take it, just count it like a turnover and hand them the ball and get back on defense. He was on point every time and literally whenever that would happen, we would turn the ball over. He had flipped out on a couple of people in the huddle; I think one of them was Druck (Nicole Druckenmiller). When she came out, she was open a few times and I think out of spite she shot the ball and ended up making it and a couple more too. So that was kind of like the turning point for us, when she started draining threes."

Another Druckenmiller three gave the Wildcats a seven-point

Villanova's Katie Davis hugs Wildcat Head Coach Harry Perretta after their stunning upset of UConn in 2003.

lead with 2:12 to go and with that Katie Davis took a bit of mental inventory on the situation.

"This is about when it started getting really crazy and exciting. You are just kind of taking it all. We are so close and I can't believe this is happening. And then you are looking at all our parents and fans in the stands and I remember looking at my mom and my dad and my dad was like 'You are in this. Keep going. Let's go.' And all of our parents were being crazy and this just got you more pumped up. So that's when I think it started to sink in that we could actually do this."

The clock kept winding down and the Wildcats kept leading and kept hitting their foul shots to keep the Huskies an arm length away. Finally, with 14 seconds left, a Jessica Moore lay-up for Connecticut made it a two-point game at 50-48. They immediately fouled, sending Juhline, an 81% free throw shooter, to the line with a chance to make it a hard-to-overcome two possession game. She would be shooting a one-and-one, meaning that if she made the first shot she would get the chance to shoot a second.

"That was the kid you wanted on the line," Perretta says.

"If she makes these, we really have a chance to win this game," Davis says. "I was a little nervous for her, but I had full confidence in her."

However, Juhline was focusing more on the "worst-case scenario" type of approach to this trip to the line – still not really believing that they were about to slay the UConn dragon.

"I was playing out in my head me missing it and them coming down and making a three and then what we were going to have to do to score. I was just like, there is no way that I'm going to make these and we are actually going to go up four and it's going to be a two possession game. I really just think it was Harry in our heads, at least in my head. He had always prepared us for things to go wrong. I guess that I was almost expecting it to happen."

Juhline would go on to prove herself wrong by burying both foul shots for her game-high 17th and 18th points of the game, giving Villanova a 52-48 lead. And then UConn committed a final turnover with 2.2 seconds remaining. And Nova Nation could exhale. And party.

"I called the play, but I never watched the play," Perretta

remembers. "I kind of saw Katie passing the ball to Trish, but as she was passing the ball to Trish, I turned my eyes and looked at the clock and I guess Trish caught it. Well, I saw the replay. Trish caught it and held it and they decided not to foul but I never looked at the play. I looked at the clock and I kept praying, 'Can it just go to zero' and it was the longest 2.2 seconds of my life. And then it went to zero and the horn went off and I turned to my associate (coach Joe Mullaney) and said, 'Did we really win?' And he said, 'Yeah, we did' and I kind of just walked out on the court in a daze."

A daze that would soon be replaced by the oncoming blur that was Katie Davis.

"(She) ran from the opposite end of the court and just jumped on me and it was kind of like this surreal feeling that it really had happened."

"I honesty don't fully remember why I decided to do that, run right to him," Davis says, "but I guess it was just spur of the moment, it's pretty funny. We have a great picture. I have it hanging on my wall."

"Once the buzzer sounded we were so excited," Mix-Davis remembers. "We weren't expecting to win, we weren't even expecting to be there. It was just so awesome. It was unbelievable."

And while the snapping of the winning streak made national news, kind of lost in the shuffle was the fact that, the Wildcats had won the Big East Championship.

"The cutting down of the nets was hysterical. It's just funny because as one of the girls on our team put it, most of us were never even high school champions," Juhline points out. "It's not like we were these dominant basketball players that were used to championships. This was, for a lot of us, the first big championship that we ever had. The streak and that kind of stuff, I guess the media was talking about that, not that we forgot, but it was like 'Oh my God we also won a championship! This is unbelievable.' And that was the coolest part. Even now, we have a championship. That's a big deal for our school and for us to have a memory of that. It's just so fun; that's really the only way I can describe it - it was so fun."

The Wildcats would really get to bask in the glory of this win because they would have almost two weeks until they would begin play in the NCAA Tournament.

"That whole week was amazing, we just were all on such a high," Davis remembers. "We were hanging out all the time together; everyone on campus was talking about it. I remember all my family members calling me, all my friends. Everyone was just super pumped about it. That time off was just amazing. Everyone could just take the time to enjoy it and celebrate."

The Wildcats would earn a #2 seed in the NCAA Tournament and advance all the way to the Elite Eight before falling to Tennessee. As it was, UConn would go on to win the National Championship for a second straight year, the loss to Villanova being the only blemish on their season.

That win that season was obviously something everyone involved will remember for a lifetime. But it's a memory that is enhanced because everyone involved just loved whom they got to do it with.

"I think the fact we were super tight and played for each other and weren't as concerned with winning is why we were able to win so many games - because that wasn't the focus. We are still super tight," Juhline says.

"We had a ton of fun. I mean, I can't explain to you how much fun that season was. Just the team, everything," Mix-Davis remembers.

"Sometimes I'll call (Juhline) on the phone and leave a message and say, 'Yeah, it really happened that night,'" Perretta says. "We think about it, we talk about it because that's what sports are supposed to be. It's supposed to be fun and we also talk about the bad games too, but it's a lot better when you talk about that game."

So what about Sister Rose Marie? Did her prayers help put this all in motion? I'll leave that for you to decide. But after the game, Coach Perretta mentioned his phone conversation on the bus during a TV interview and that set in motion an interesting string of events.

"When I got to see Sister Rose Marie in June, I get to see her once a year, she said, 'You know it was really funny but, since the game was played, they (the monastery) were getting phone calls from different teams in the country. College, high school, grade school teams were all calling the monastery asking them to pray for their team to win the championship.' She also told me that there was actually a reporter from the Washington Post who came up and knocked on the door of the monastery wanting to interview her. Now you have to remember something; they are cloistered so they don't talk to ANYBODY. Mother Superior didn't understand the whole thing, so I had to explain it to her why all these people were calling to get prayers. Because we may be one of the biggest upsets in women's basketball history."

Skip Wilson

"As you look back on things, maybe I should have gone to baseball right away."

– SKIP WILSON ON SPLITTING TIME IN HIS YOUNGER YEARS BETWEEN BASEBALL AND BASKETBALL

46 years is a long time to do anything. As I write this, I have been at the station going on 8 years, which is four times longer than I've been at any other job in the business. The idea of being at one place, doing one job for more than four and a half decades, is just incredible to me. But that's the story of longtime Temple baseball coach James "Skip" Wilson, who piloted the Owls baseball team from 1960 to 2005. But he did much, much more than just stick around for nearly half a century. Wilson would win 1,034 games over his career, have 23 players selected in the Major League Baseball draft, qualify for the NCAA Tournament 13 times and advance to the College World Series twice. He would have such an impact on the Temple program that his number (#6) would be retired in 2007, a year after the Owls home field in Ambler, PA was named after him.

While baseball eventually became his bread and butter, in his younger days, Wilson's athletic allegiances were split between baseball and basketball. Growing up in Philadelphia, Wilson went to La Salle High School for two years and then transferred to St. John's High in Manayunk. As a youngster, Wilson's athletic prowess started to really get some attention.

TEMPLE UNIVERSITY ATHLETICS

Skip Wilson talks strategy with his Owls on the mound.

"Chief Bender, the old pitcher (and Baseball Hall of Famer), saw me playing in the sandlots and he got me down to work out with the (Philadelphia) A's all the time and my father thought I had a great future."

Wilson was turning heads as a middle infielder. He got tryouts with the Brooklyn Dodgers and the Detroit Tigers, and the A's kept an eye on him, but he decided to go to college to play basketball. A point guard, he would first go to Georgetown and then transfer to Stetson University. But he soon left school and jumped back into baseball, playing in the low minors of the A's organization. After a stint in the military, he returned to the A's organization and he says they gave him a contract to play in the Class C Evangeline League down in New Iberia, Louisiana.

"I went down there, that's in the bayou, and the mosquitoes were as big as your fist."

And all it took was a week down there to convince Wilson it was time to come back home and get his degree. He decided to go to

Temple. Then, one day in 1956, Wilson embarked on his coaching career, but his interview process turned out to be a little . . . informal.

"I was playing basketball one day with (Temple legends) "Pickles" Kennedy and Guy Rodgers and the athletic director saw me and asked, 'How come you're not out for the team?' And I said my eligibility was over a long while ago."

But Wilson saw an opportunity and quickly asked about the job opening the athletic department had for a freshman basketball coach.

"He said, 'Do you know anything about it?' I said, 'I know quite a bit about the game.' Tell (Head basketball coach) Harry Litwack you are now his new freshman (basketball) coach.' So I went and told Harry, but he said they already had somebody. So I took a shower and was leaving when the Athletic Director, Mr. Josh Cody, saw me and said, 'Where are you going?'"

Wilson informed him that Coach Litwack said the position had already been filled.

"He said, 'Go back up there and tell him he has dual coaches now.' That's how I got hired - on the basketball court."

Wilson would spent three years solely coaching that freshman basketball team, but then prior to the 1959 baseball season, when he was riding in a limousine on his way to New York for an event honoring Coach Litwack, he had a conversation with Cody about a new opportunity.

"Mr. Cody knew he was retiring and the baseball coach (Ernie Casale) was going to become the AD. So he told me, 'Skippy, I want you to be the assistant baseball coach this year.' I said, 'Mr. Cody, I'm a basketball coach, I don't want to coach baseball.' He said, 'I want you to be the baseball coach.' Emphatically. So I said ok. I was the assistant coach for a year and then I had the job."

Wilson's first season in charge of the baseball team was 1960 (he would remain an assistant basketball coach as well until 1972) and he made a smooth transition. His Owls went 16-5.

"What happened the first year is I had three very good pitchers. And we breezed right through."

Year two saw Wilson not have that type of pitching, and the Owls slumped to 6-11-1. However, that proved to be a very brief bump in the road, as Wilson soon found his pace and Temple became a team to be reckoned with in the Northeast. The rest of the decade would feature four 20-win seasons with three of those campaigns featuring winning percentages of .800 or better. Two times Wilson's Owls would advance to the NCAA Tournament, first in 1963 and then again in 1968. As successful as the first ten years of Wilson's coaching career were, they would prove to be really just a warm-up for a run of excellence that was just around the corner.

While the 1970 and 1971 seasons were nothing to write home about, the Temple baseball program would be taken to a new level in 1972. Under Wilson's tutelage, the Owls won a then school-record 33 games and claimed the MAC Championship. Once again, they advanced to the NCAA Tournament and soon moved on to the College World Series, but not without a little luck. Wilson recalls a tournament game with Penn State that was tight in the late innings. The Nittany Lions had the bases loaded with nobody out and a 3-0 count on the batter. The fourth pitch looked to be sailing way inside to force in a critical run, but as the batter backed out of the way, the errant pitch hit the knob of the bat. It bounced right to the pitcher who, of course, started a 1-2-3 double play to take the steam out of the Penn State rally. The Owls held on to win and headed to Omaha, Nebraska for the Series.

"You gotta be lucky," Wilson recalls with a smile.

The Owls were anything but just happy to be there, as they announced their presence with authority at the 1972 College World Series. After a 13-inning 2-1 loss to Oklahoma in the first game of the double elimination tournament, the Owls bounced back to take Iowa 13-9, eliminating the Hawkeyes. The next day, they sent Connecticut home after handing them their second loss 7-4. Following a day off, Wilson's squad would go toe-to-toe with one of the most storied programs in college baseball history, Arizona State. Temple more than held their own before losing 1-0.

That '72 team, despite finishing third in the CWS, did not get a single player named to the All-Tournament team. And while this may be a tip of the hat toward the coaching job Wilson did, don't think this group was without its special players. Perhaps the most notable was right-hander Joe Kerrigan, who would have a modest Major League career as a player but really make his name as one of the game's great pitching coaches. Wilson would use him as the closer on that World Series team.

"This was long before colleges were using closers. But I had Kerrigan as the closer, and when I put him in, it was pretty well over because I would bring him in the 8th and 9th innings."

"I think I was one of the youngest players, if not the youngest, player to ever pitch in a College World Series at that time (18) and I remember pitching well in relief. Good enough to get a save and a win out of the two wins we got there," Kerrigan says. "You were playing against the cream of the crop there. Several of those teams had players that went on to have long careers in the big leagues. The Fred Lynns (USC), the Bump Wills (Arizona State) and Craig Swans (Arizona State). It was about as good a competition as you can get."

Kerrigan was not just a baseball player for Wilson, but he also had had him as a mentor on the hardwood.

"I hope people realize he was an equally good or maybe better basketball coach than he was a baseball coach. He was a guy who was very passionate. Loved both sports, very demanding of his players,"Kerrigan remembers. "(Wilson) loved intelligent players, guys who knew what they were doing on the field and on the court. And he demanded that you knew the game and I learned at a young age that you better play attention, you better be at the right place at the right time and you better understand what's going on around you during the game. And for that I owe him a lot."

The mid-70s saw more good baseball at Temple, with Wilson's squad returning to the NCAA Tournament in 1973, 1975 and 1976. Ed Hayes was a right-handed pitcher on the '75 and '76 teams. He would go on to become a lawyer, later representing many Owls who made it into pro ball. He would also become a close friend of his college coach.

"He really took the time to teach you fundamentals. Took the time to be sure that everyone took a team approach to the game and when you combine all of those things, despite the fact that we were a northeastern team that got a late start compared to everyone else, we played the game fundamentally well. We had a lot of talent and Skip had a way of really bringing it all together to really create a special program."

The good times for Temple continued in 1977, as talent and a little bit of luck came together to get the Owls back to the College World Series.

Wilson had assembled a team that went 34-9 and at one point had won 23 of 24 games. That was the talent part. The luck part came in the NCAA Tournament's Northeast regional up in Middletown, Connecticut. The Owls were trying to hold on to an 8-6 lead in the 8th inning against Cornell, but the Big Red had loaded the bases with no outs. Things looked even worse when a line drive exploded off the bat of a Cornell batter, destined to turn the game around . . . except that it landed right in the glove of shortstop Pete Dempsey, who turned it into a line drive triple play. Ball game.

"After the game, I go down to the hotel bar," Wilson remembers. "I'm having a beer and who is sitting there but the coach from Cornell. And I said to the bartender, 'Send the fellow over there a drink and before he gets too upset tell him we practice that play every day.'"

Temple's second appearance in the College World Series would be much shorter and much less successful than their first trip in 1972. The Owls lost their first game to Southern Illinois and their second

Skip Wilson (left) watches his Owls from the dugout.

TEMPLE UNIVERSITY ATHLETICS

to Clemson, finishing 8th in the eight team field. One of the key players on this team was lefthander Pete Filson. Despite being just a freshman in '77, he played an important role on the Owls pitching staff.

"It was a great experience," Filson says. "We didn't perform, me included, as well as we would have hoped to. But a lot of times it's the journey getting there."

Filson would go on to be drafted by the Yankees and pitch seven seasons in the majors. He looks back at his time under Wilson fondly.

"Skip loved to win. That was probably the main thing. Skip was pretty intense, but off the field he was a fun loving guy. He was, I'd say, easy for me to play for because he'd give me the ball. Can't ask for more than that."

While Wilson's Owls would never return to the College World

Series, they would continue to win and he would continue to develop Major League talent. From 1980 to 1989, the Owls would win at least 25 games every season and make three appearances in the NCAA Tournament. And some, if not the greatest, hitters that Wilson would ever coach would come on the scene during these years.

Wilson calls John Marzano the best pure hitter he ever coached. A catcher from Philadelphia's Central High, Marzano's career under Wilson began in 1982. His Temple career would lead to a 1984 US Olympic team berth, a first round selection in the Major League draft and a long career as a solid back-up catcher. He came to North Broad Street a gifted hitter, but Wilson says his defense needed work and he was never shy of reminding him about it.

"We were playing Rhode Island one time and must have been 20 scouts there for him. First inning hits a home run, in the 3rd or 4th inning hits another home run, drives in a couple more. 7th inning drives in a couple more. 3 home runs, drove in 7 or 8 of the runs. But in the interim he had two or three errors. Passed balls. Overthrows. THEY scored 5-6 runs. On the third home run, he came around, I'm coaching third, he says, 'Don't you ever say anything?' and I said, 'No and I didn't say anything about those errors either.' And I said, 'Get your ass over there and shut up or all those scouts back there won't know who you are sitting on the bench with me this next game.'"

Needless to say, the scouts still got to watch Marzano. Honest moments like this one helped catcher and coach forge a deep friendship that lasted until Marzano's untimely death in 2008 at the age of 45.

"I really liked him as a person, not only as a ballplayer. John and I were very close."

Marzano would not be the first, nor the last, of Wilson's former players to become a friend.

"I got along pretty well with most of them because I treated them like men. They were no longer boys. They weren't teenagers anymore. And I used to say to them, 'I'm going to treat you like a man until you show me you want to be treated like a boy. Then I'll treat you like a boy.' I never wanted to be a cop."

A year after Marzano came to Temple, Wilson recruited a pitcher from Bristol High named Jeff Manto. Well, at least he was a pitcher when he CAME to Temple. Wilson says, about a day and a half into his Owl career, he moved Manto to the outfield.

"He couldn't throw strikes."

Like Marzano, Manto would prove to be a great college hitter. In fact, they are the top two hitters in Temple history. Both players actually hit .413 as Owls but "technically" Marzano hit .4130 while Manto came in at .4127. Wilson says he knew Manto was special by his sophomore year.

"When he started hitting home runs and he made all the plays in the outfield and if you tug up on him he was going to throw you out. If you tried to go to third, he would throw you out. He has such a good arm. And then he was around John and the two of them, they made you a very special team."

Manto would go on to play parts of nine seasons in the majors after being selected by the Angels in the 14th round of the MLB draft in 1985.

The Manto and Marzano years would indeed be good ones for Wilson's program; the two helped lead the Owls to Atlantic 10 Championships and berths in the NCAA Tournament in 1983 and 1984. Those teams would be anchored on the mound by Billy Mendek. He would prove to be one of the most dominant pitchers Wilson would coach. In fact, if Wilson had to pick a pitcher from his years to win one game for all the marbles, he says Mendek would be it. He still holds the Temple record for career wins with 30 and is also second all-time in saves. He would be drafted by Seattle in 1984 and get as high as Triple A.

Wilson continued to pile up the victories — the 1985 Owls would win 34 games, the most for the program since the 1977 CWS team.

As the 80s came to a close, Wilson would bring in another big time bat to the Temple program, a young man arriving from Frankford High in 1989.

"You can tell the special ones. Bobby Higginson was special," Wilson remembers. "I didn't know that at first. He came as a second base-man and I hit him maybe ten ground balls that first day or two he was there and his hands were like (as he points to a wall) that wall. I was like get the hell out in the outfield. So I put him out in right-field because he had a gun and that's how he got to the outfield."

Skip Wilson won 1,034 games during his time as Temple's baseball coach.

TEMPLE UNIVERSITY ATHLETICS

Higginson would become one of the greatest outfielders in Owl history, setting a program record with 30 home runs (since broken) and finish his career with a .371 batting average. He would be drafted by the Tigers in 1992 and go on to put together a wonderful 11-year Major League career which included 187 home runs.

The 90s would prove to be leanest of Wilson's years at Temple. He says rumors that the University might drop baseball as a varsity sport in the early part of the decade made recruiting that much tougher. From 1990 to 1999, the Owls had only two .500 or better seasons and they would qualify for the Atlantic 10 Tournament just three times.

The Owls may not have been winning as often as Wilson would like, but his players would continue to improve individually. Wilson says being on the field with the players, laughing with them and teaching them, was his favorite part of the job.

"I really enjoyed watching a kid progress. I really enjoyed watching kids come in as freshmen, young men and going out mature."

For the most part, Wilson says he tried to keep it simple when it came to his coaching.

"I'd come home from a game and if my team made a mistake I'd put it on a 3 x 5 card. That night I would make a drill up for that mistake and the next day we went over that drill. Then nobody could say, 'I never knew that.' Now you know it because I just taught it to you."

Temple fans probably didn't think that the 2001 season was going to be one to remember either. Wilson's Owls went winless on a season opening road trip, dragging an 0-14 record into their home opener with Lehigh. But despite the big hole, the cagey field general was confident that this team would dig out of it.

"I had a heck of a group. We lost 14 games in a row in California, but I knew we were good. We went on to win the conference championship."

That Atlantic 10 championship carried with it the program's first NCAA Tournament appearance since 1984.

"We went back to California and played the #1 team in the country. We came home very quickly."

The Owls lost to Cal-State Fullerton and Texas Tech to get eliminated, but this group had returned the Owl program to national prominence.

That would prove to be the last real high point for Wilson's Owls over his final years as coach. He would retire in 2005, finishing his career with those remarkable 1,034 wins against 824 losses for a .556 winning percentage.

"I miss the mental part of it. Yeah, I do miss baseball because I always thought that I could teach basic fundamentals."

While he may not be coaching anymore, the friendships forged during his decades at Temple are as strong as ever.

"They were my family and I treated them like my sons. I treated them the way I wanted to be treated and I have had them over the course of the time I have been retired say that to me. They say you always treated us like men. You allowed us to grow up."

One of those former players, Hayes, spearheaded the drive to get the Owls field in Ambler named after his college coach.

"I just think he was always a genuine person who always had the players' best interest at hand. To me, his players were the single most important thing in the world to him, both from the standpoint from what you were doing on the field and what you were doing in school and what you were doing personally. And that's just something that always stuck with me."

Nick Allen and Kevin Mulvey

"I hadn't thrown a ball yet that day and I just told him 'something good's going to happen today.'"

– NICK ALLEN ON A CONVERSATION WITH
CATCHER ANDY WENDLE

One of the really great things about baseball is the possibility of something special happening when you least expect it. Like when the Phillies' Steve Jeltz – the man who only had 1 home run in 1,100 or so Major League at-bats - hit home runs from both sides of the plate in a 15-11 win over the Pirates back in 1989. I know that's random, but I try to work Steve Jeltz's name into the conversation wherever I can. The point is that you just never know what's going to happen. And that's why we care.

As of February 25th, 2005, there had been six no-hitters thrown in the history of Villanova baseball. The most recent was back in 1962, when two gentlemen named Bruce Howard and Mike Kiley combined for one in a 22-0 win over Philadelphia Textile (now Philadelphia University). So needless to say, when the Wildcats prepared for a doubleheader down in Norfolk, Virginia against winless Norfolk State on February 26th, history wasn't on many people's minds, except maybe senior right-hander Nick Allen.

"I was running with (catcher) Andy Wendle before I even threw my bullpen to get ready for the game," Allen says. "I hadn't thrown

STEVE ALLEN

Nick Allen threw one of two Villanova no-hitters back in 2005.

a ball yet that day and I just told him, 'Something good's going to happen today.'"

Boy did it.

Norfolk got a runner on in the second on an error, but Allen induced a double play to end the inning. In the third, Norfolk would threaten. Allen hit the leadoff man, who promptly stole second and advanced to third on a Wendle throwing error. Even without a hit, the Spartans were in position to score the game's first run. But the threat seemed to embolden Allen, who struck out the next two hitters before getting a ground ball to second to end the frame.

The next three innings saw Allen retire all nine hitters he faced with just one ball leaving the infield, and history's spider sense was tingling.

"I think in the fourth and fifth inning when my teammates stopped sitting next to me I realized something was going on," Allen admits, "and I got a little excited - but tried to keep it under control."

The Wildcats scratched out single runs in the top of the 6th and

7th innings to take a 2-0 lead into the bottom of the seventh – keep in mind that in college baseball, games of a doubleheader are seven innings in length. Now all eyes were on the 6-1, 190 pound senior from Green Lane, Pennsylvania who stood alone on the hill. Three outs away from history.

"It's on your mind... I don't care what people say, it's on your mind. You know what is going on, you know the other team hasn't gotten a hit yet."

Allen started the inning by getting the Norfolk catcher on a called third strike. One out. Then it was a ground ball to third. Two outs. Spartan third baseman Juan Serrano stepped in, as determined to wreck history as Allen was to make it.

Allen delivered, Serrano swung and two words ran through the Wildcat right hander's mind.

"Oh sh*t."

Serrano hit a slicing line drive to right field, but Al Day was playing shallow and made the catch and the celebration was on.

"It's a complete blur. I remember Al catching it and I think Andy was already right out at the mound hugging me so I didn't really have that much time to take it all in and see anything," Allen admits.

History had been made. It would be repeated exactly one month later.

Sophomore Kevin Mulvey took the mound on March 26th, 2005 against Connecticut at the Wildcats' home field in Plymouth Meeting, looking to keep the train rolling. The Wildcats had won six of seven as they moved towards the heart of the Big East schedule, and the right-hander would get the ball for the first game of a doubleheader against the Huskies. At this point, it had been a full month since a Wildcat had thrown a no-hitter, and everyone was hungry for more history. Mulvey did not disappoint.

"Yeah, I felt pretty good coming out of the bullpen," Mulvey would say then. "I don't know about no-hitter stuff. But I felt good."

Allen, now a no-hitter veteran, was charting Mulvey's pitches that day.

"They had no chance against him that day. He was dominant."

Mulvey, a native of Parlin, NJ, retired the first nine batters he faced and allowed just one walk through six innings. That mistake was eliminated on a double play in the fourth. Baseball players are about as superstitious as they come. So as Mulvey was making short work of the Huskies, Allen was doing his best to avoid the obvious.

"I was sitting next to Rick Clagett, our pitching coach, and we were trying to just keep going with our usual banter without saying too much. Because you know how we are about superstition."

Mulvey was more focused on the job at hand than on history.

"I was just trying to keep runners off base and to try and win the game. I was just trying to get outs and it just so happen that nobody got a hit."

The only semblance of trouble came in the final inning, as Mulvey had to dance between a leadoff walk and another base-on-balls in the frame. But he secured his spot in the record book with a fielder's choice to shortstop Ryan Arcadia. Mulvey had no hit the Huskies and needed just an hour and twenty-one minutes to do it.

One common thread in the two no-no's - Andy Wendle caught both of them. And he says the two hurlers took different paths to the same place in history.

"Kevin's stuff was that good and he threw that hard some days and it moved that much sometimes that it was just 'come and hit me if you can,'" Wendle says. "With Nick it was a lot more thoughtful, a lot more thought out, a lot more with scouting reports."

"I was so excited and nervous at the same time for Nick," Mulvey says. "And then when I was throwing you know I'm excited. Not really nervous, but kind of thinking about it as you go on toward the last inning, the last two innings like 'Wow this could happen' and it's just awesome that it did!"

Nick Allen and Kevin Mulvey

Both Allen and Mulvey would use their Villanova careers to elevate them to the pros. Allen was selected in the 21st round by Seattle following his senior season of 2005. Mulvey would actually be a second round pick of the Mets, 62nd overall, in 2006. He was the Mets' top selection, making him the only Villanova player ever taken with a team's first draft choice.

Allen would last three years in the Mariners' system, getting as high as the High-A High Desert Mavericks of the California League. He now works in the financial sector down in Charlotte, NC.

Mulvey is now with the Arizona Diamondbacks' organization. The Mets traded him to Minnesota in 2008 as part of the package that brought ace lefthander Johan Santana to the Big Apple, and he made his Major League debut with the Twins in July of 2009. Two months later he was dealt to Arizona.

And I would be remiss here if I didn't mention Mike Loree. Two days before Mulvey provided the back-end bookend to no-hit history, Loree, in a way, actually bested both Allen and Mulvey. He went 7 1/3 innings without allowing a hit in a 3-1 win over Rutgers. This was a nine inning game, however, so Loree was lifted after the knock and had to "settle" for being one of three pitchers to take part in just the fifth Wildcat one-hitter in history and the first in 13 years.

A post post-script. The San Francisco Giants would draft Loree in the 50th round in 2007. And in 2008 he put together one of the most mind-blowing stretches a pitcher has had. Hurling for the Giants Short-Season A squad, the Salem-Keizer Volcanoes, he retired 62 of 63 batters he faced in a span of four starts. Over 21 innings, one guy reached base. One guy. He got the final two outs of one start, then twirled six perfect innings next time out. He followed that up by retiring the first 20 batters in his next start before allowing a home run (the one guy to reach base). He got the final out that night and then finished the amazing run with seven perfect innings in the next game. Yes, that Villanova pitching staff wasn't too shabby at all.

Jack Childs came to Drexel after a successful career as head coach at Stevens Trade (now Stevens College of Technology) in Lancaster.

Jack Childs

"If they come, they come. I'm not concerned about that. I'm concerned about developing these young guys."

– JACK CHILDS ON MILESTONES

I t is absolutely no surprise that Drexel wrestling coach Jack Childs was a three-sport star at Athens Area High School in Bradford County, PA. What is surprising for the active leader in career Division One wrestling coaching victories - is that wrestling was not one of those three sports.

"We didn't have wrestling in my high school until my senior year," Childs says. "We did have a wrestling club and during gym class I would go to the wrestling club and wrestle, get to know the rudiments of it just because I liked it. But I had always played football and track and to stay in shape for track, I would play basketball. And I lettered all four years in all three sports."

But despite his relatively late introduction to the sport, Coach Childs has become an institution during his 34 years at Drexel, a legend in the ranks of wrestling coaches and a Hall of Famer.

After graduating from Athens Area High, Childs went to Ithaca College on a football and track scholarship. As a requisite for majoring in physical education, Childs had to go out for an intramural sport. He chose wrestling and became the heavyweight wrestling champ. It is here that our story begins to come together. Shortly after returning from Christmas break, Childs says he was approached by the Ithaca wrestling coach, who was in desperate need of a freshman heavyweight to replace the one he had just thrown off the team.

"I said, 'Coach I've got a heavy load. I'm getting ready for spring ball plus track is coming up. I really don't have the time.' He said, 'What are you having problems with as far as your course load is concerned?'"

Childs pointed out his struggles with his gymnastics class.

"I said, 'I can't get over that damn long horse for anything and the parallel bars are killing me'. He said, 'Come out for wrestling and you'll get a pass through for the gymnastics.' So I went out for wrestling. We had seven matches and I went 4-2-1. They had draws then, and really enjoyed the sport. So that's how I got into it."

Childs returned to Ithaca for his sophomore year, but soon a steep hike in tuition at the school forced him to transfer to East Stroudsburg, a school he had been accepted to before he decided on Ithaca. As a result of the transfer, Childs would have to sit out a year before he could compete in any sport.

"But when they called for the wrestlers in September, I thought, 'Well heck, this would be a great way to get in shape for spring football'. So I went out for wrestling. I was eligible in January and wrestled half the year and did get in shape for football, but I was kind of hooked on wrestling."

Childs calls himself an average wrestler – his high water mark was a third place finish in the Pennsylvania State Championships one year. But the sport had become an important part of his life.

He would graduate from college in 1967 and there was little doubt which direction he wanted to go from there.

"I knew I wanted to coach when I graduated; that's why I was studying health and physical education."

His first job would take him to a high school in Fulton, New York, where he would serve as assistant head wrestling coach and also the head coach of the junior high football and track teams. A year later, he moved over to Binghamton Central High to become the head wrestling and assistant football and track coach. Childs would spend two years there before heading back to Pennsylvania to become head wrestling and assistant track and football coach at Stevens Trade School in Lancaster (now the Stevens College of Technology).

This would be Childs' final stop before coming to Drexel – a move which almost didn't happen. He would spend six years at Stevens, shedding his track responsibilities after three. His wrestling program flourished, his squad going 89-17. He also drew some interest on the football front he says, turning down coordinator offers from schools like Franklin and Marshall and Millersville. It was during his fourth year that he was first in contact with Drexel about an opening as head wrestling coach. But he says circumstances kept him in Lancaster – for now.

"My wife was pregnant with our first son, Jesse. We were 25 minutes from her mother, we had her doctor there and it just was not the right time. I was offered the position but did not take it."

Childs' wrestling squad continued to dominate at Stevens and the next year the wrestling gig at Drexel once again came open.

"And I put in for it but they said, believe it or not, the money was less then, than they had offered me the year before. And we had already started our family and I told them I was not going to be able to take the position."

Childs remained at Stevens and was happy, and it looked as if the Drexel window had closed. I mean, who gets three chances to take the same job? Well . . .

The coach Drexel hired when Childs declined the job didn't work out, to say the least, and was let go after just a few months. So would the third time be the charm? Given what you know about this story already, the answer is pretty obvious. But work with me. The parting of the ways with that coach actually left the Dragon program in turmoil. No coach meant no team, and Drexel actually played host to the East Coast Conference Championships in 1976 sans a team of their own.

"So I was contacted again. And I said, 'I've been over there twice, I don't need to come over for an interview. If you're serious about it you'll offer me the job'. They did."

The money was still an issue, however then Athletic Director John Semanik was able to get the numbers where Childs needed them, and in 1976 Drexel would announce they had a new head wrestling coach.

Childs would have his work cut out for him that first year. Of course, the school hadn't fielded a team the year before, but the program had really been struggling even before that. It hadn't had a winning season in nine years. Childs was looking for talent anywhere he could find it.

"I went through the dorms. I looked at the admission rolls. I saw where kids were from. I looked over what they had and you've got to realize that Drexel at that time only had about 6000 students. It was not a huge university at that time. I got guys out of the dorms. There were two guys from Western PA that had applied, and I got in touch with them and they were all set to go to another school, and they came to Drexel."

Childs was impressive that first year, compiling a 6-5-1 record which turned enough heads for him to finish second in the Amateur Wrestling News Rookie Coach of the Year balloting. Who was the man who beat him out for the award? Dan Gable at Iowa. If wrestling has a "rock star", it's Dan Gable. He of the 118-1 career wrestling mark at Iowa State and the 15 NCAA Titles as a coach at Iowa. Childs has been running in elite circles from Jump Street at Drexel.

That first season was just the beginning of a slew of special moments and seasons at Drexel, each showing that Childs was putting his stamp on the program.

"I think of the first wrestler that ever went to the nationals for me, Keith Wenger, a heavyweight. It was my fifth year here (1980). It took us five years to really get the program where I had a boy that would be able to compete on the national level, and that was out in Oregon."

The team would get better and better and then in 1985, it all came together. Childs and his Dragons had an East Coast Conference Championship in their sights.

"We went 15-1 that year. We lost to Rider and championships were at Hofstra. We were tied with Rider and our heavyweight had to win, and if he won we were the champions," Childs remembers. "Lo and behold he wins and we win the conference championship. And Gary Taylor, good friend of mine who is still coaching at Rider said to me, 'You know I'd trade that win that we had over you in the dual match for this championship', and I said, 'You're not going to get that.'"

After winning that championship, as the team returned to Philadelphia by bus, Coach Childs informed them that he was going to take them out for a big dinner to celebrate. However, the coach says his squad wanted to keep it simple instead.

"So we went to White Castle."

Childs still looks back on that 1985 group fondly.

"They are probably the most determined and as hard working a group as I've had."

As the years passed, the victories accumulated with Childs methodically moving up the career coaching lists. On January 17th, 2002, he picked up his 300th Division I win as his Dragons defeated rival Rider.

"Beating (Rider Head Coach) Gary Taylor is always a pleasure," Childs says with a smile.

By now Childs was not just incredibly successful, but his imprint both on Drexel and the sport of wrestling itself was well known. So much so that in 2006, Childs learned he was going to be inducted into the National Wrestling Hall of Fame in Stillwater, Oklahoma as a Lifetime Achievement Award recipient.

"To be recognized by your peers, it was overwhelming. I was humbled by it. The people that you are associated with when you are on that level... it's the wrestling world. It was something that you take and reflect on and go on from there."

If the Hall of Fame induction had one challenge, it was the speech that Childs had to give at the awards banquet held in Reading by the Pennsylvania Chapter of the National Hall of Fame.

"How do you give acclaim to everybody who has helped you to get to that position?"

Childs pulled it off and that evening would provide a snapshot into just how much Childs has influenced the lives of his wrestlers. He proudly points to a photo from that night.

"Sixteen of my wrestlers came - only two of them were wrestling for me at the time. The other 14 came because of the relationship we had. I did not know, other than my two sons, I didn't know anyone else was going to be there so it was quite an affair."

In recent years, Childs has continued to accumulate victories and to see his program grow. In fact, his first two All-Americans emerged in the last five years. In 2004, 125-pounder Robbie Rebmann, in Childs' words a "real tough nut", was poised to earn the coveted NCAA All-American status, which means a top 8 finish at Nationals. In order to do that however, Rebmann was going to have to beat a wrestler that had already bested him three times that season, Tom Noto from Hofstra.

"And they are tied at the end of regulation, so it goes into sudden death. Take down is a victory. My boy shoots in, gets on the single leg and I saw where he was and I stood up and I said, 'It's over'. And lo and behold he converts that single leg to the takedown and we knew he was an All-American then. I mean the emotion, the tears, it all came at one time."

All-American number #2 came three years later, a special talent by the name of Ryan Hluschak. While Drexel originally recruited him out of high school, Hluschak went to Lehigh on a football scholarship. But soon he decided that he really missed wrestling and reached out to Coach Childs, who was in need of a 157-pounder - which just happened to be Hluschak's weight class.

"That showed me what kind of a guy Coach Childs was. He told me prior to my senior year when I told him the disappointing news that I wasn't going to go with Drexel - for him to tell me then that the door would always be open and to actually confirm that a year later - told me he was a straight shooter kind of guy, and what kind of person he was."

Hluschak would go on to litter his name throughout the Drexel wrestling book, setting a program record with 121 career victories (A record broken in 2010 by Steve Mytych). Perhaps his biggest win came at Nationals in Auburn Hills, Michigan in March of 2007. Hluschak was matching up with a talented grappler named Brian Stith out of Arizona State. Moments before that match, Hluschak says the two had a conversation which showed exactly why Childs is the active leader in Division I coaching victories.

"Most of my matches at that tournament, prior to the round of 12, crucial All-American match, were very high scoring, where I was kind of going out and letting it hang out. He knew what kind of opponent I had and that I wasn't going to be able to get away with exposing myself by trying to go out there and do everything I could to score a lot of points. He pretty much said this match is going to have to be different, you're going to have to play it safe, conservative, and then wait for that one moment and go."

Hluschak says his sage coach was right on the money. He followed his advice, beat Stith, and in turn became Drexel's second All-American.

"The strategy I had intended to use definitely wouldn't have worked and his saying that right before I went on, when all previous six matches I had wrestled out there. I had wrestled totally opposite of that way. So for him to have that intuition and sort of strategic insight and to relay it to me in that crucial situation and for me to deploy it and to be successful in the deployment was something I'll never forget."

Like many of the wrestlers to come through the Drexel program, Hluschak stays in touch with Childs. The two talk trout fishing and touch base about once a month. It's no surprise that Drexel wrestlers stay in touch with Coach Childs, because he knows what he is looking for when he recruits kids into the program. And it goes beyond talent on the mat.

"When I go to watch at a match or a tournament, I like to watch how they warm up. I like to see how they prepare mentally. I also like to see how they accord themselves after the match is over. If they won, are they pompous or are they a gentleman? Do they just shake hands and go and slap the guy on the back and go off to the side or do they celebrate insanely? That person, you know, I want to check and see where he is. Of course if they lose and they throw a tantrum or a fit or anything, then they really have to look inside themselves. I want to see them a couple more times. I don't care how good the athlete may be, there are some guys I have just shied away from. They are not going to fit in at Drexel and they are not going to fit into my program here. We've kind of made it like a family oriented program."

Ain't that the truth. All three of Childs' children attended Drexel and were outstanding athletes. His daughter Elizabeth captained the tennis team, while sons Jesse and Mike both wrestled for their dad. But their connection to the program started even before they put on the Dragon singlet.

"I have a lot of great memories growing up when I was little just going on road trips with my brother," Mike Childs remembers. "Being so little that we could fall asleep on the bus. Jesse and I would fall asleep on the luggage rack. We would put our coats up there and we were small enough to fit and we would go up to Boston or down to

Baltimore. I have great memories of doing that. Meeting all the wrestlers — when you're seven, eight, nine, college-aged kids seem so old and so cool. Those are great memories for me."

Mike and Jesse made their way onto the wrestling team in the mid 90's after graduating from Radnor High, and the boys and their dad were together for three years. Jesse wrestled at 150 while Mike shifted between 150, 157 and 165. Jesse remembers his first collegiate match. After red-shirting as a freshman, Childs made his debut at the Bloomsburg Open as a sophomore, wrestling a senior from VMI.

"I'm not known to be a strong guy; I was more of a thin, wiry 150-pounder. And here I am wrestling this cement block of a cadet from VMI who placed fourth the year before. I fought off my back pretty much the first and second periods and I got on top the third period and I rode him pretty well, and was trying to turn him and I got off the mat and I lost by a slim margin. I think it might have been 5-1 or something, and my dad looked at me with a tear in his eye and he's like, 'Welcome to college. Good match.' You know, I will always remember that."

Coaching a child can be a tricky balancing act. Where does coach stop and dad begin? But both Jesse and Mike applaud the way dad handled their years together.

"My dad and I are best friends. So I have a great relationship with him," Jesse says, "and it made it really easy. He treated me like one of the guys."

While Jesse has gone into technology sales, Mike has followed dad's lead and spent several years coaching wrestling here in the states, and even spent a stint overseas in Scotland. Needless to say, his father's excellence has influenced him.

"He introduced me to the sport and it's the sport that I love. The interactions that he's had with his student athletes, I've always kind of admired that. The educational role and the coaching role, he's great at it. I certainly learned a lot from him."

The wins and milestones continued to pile up after both his sons graduated. Childs hit the 400-win mark at Drexel in 2009. While the hope was to reach that remarkable milestone at home, instead it came January 17th in Fairfax, Virginia on the campus of George Mason University at the CAA Duals. Sacred Heart was the victim, the Dragons rolling 34-9.

"We had a lot of parents there, the guys all came around and congratulations were given out and pictures were taken and it was nice," Childs remembers.

Childs picked up his 500th career coaching win (including his time at Stevens) on January 23rd, 2010, his Dragons taking care of George Mason. He now stands 5th on the All-Time College Wrestling Coaching Win list. That's at any level. Let's touch on some accomplishments I've failed to bring up at this point. Childs has posted double-digit wins in 23 of his campaigns at Drexel, been named the East Coast Wrestling Association Coach of the Year four times (1980, 85, 94 and 99), and he was the CAA's Co-Coach of the Year in 2002. The 65-year-old Childs enjoyed his 34th season at the helm of the Dragons in 2009-10. We've gone over an incredible resume. So, has retirement crossed his mind at all? He says it has. But...

"Right now I enjoy recruiting. We have a great product to sell here at Drexel. The enthusiasm certainly hasn't waned. I do have two grandchildren that I dearly love and that has been a new experience for me and there's going to be a time where I'm going to want to spend more time with them. But just when that time comes I won't say now."

Neither will I.

Delaware Valley College Wrestling

"It's a brand name now.
It's a tradition now and kids
come here because they
want to be a part of it."

– HEAD COACH BRANDON TOTTEN
ON THE AGGIE PROGRAM

I t was early 1970. Richard Nixon was working on year number two of his first presidential term. Len Dawson had just led the upstart Kansas City Chiefs to a win in the final Super Bowl before the AFL/NFL merger. Simon and Garfunkel were at the top of the charts with the song "Bridge Over Troubled Waters" and in Doylestown, Pennsylvania the Delaware Valley College wrestling team lost its final dual meet of the season to Wilkes, to cap a 5-7 campaign. Not a terrible year, but in retrospect it has turned out to be extraordinarily noteworthy. Why? Because it's the last losing season the Aggie program has had.

Following the 1968-69 wrestling season, Delaware Valley was looking for a new head coach. During the search process, they contacted Robert Marshall, a standout wrestler at Purdue who at that time was the Head Wrestling Coach at Dickinson College in Carlisle.

"Del Val had wanted me to come there for a couple of years," Marshall remembers, "but then they called me this one time and asked if I was interested and I said no, I wasn't."

Robert Marshall (center) was the architect of the Delaware Valley College wrestling program. Here he is being honored at DVC with former college president Dr. Thomas C. Leamer (left) and current president Dr. Joseph S. Brosnan (right).

He was quickly asked if he had a name he could give them of another possible candidate.

"I said there is only one person I would recommend and it was my brother. Within a week they had him moved down there."

Floyd Marshall would coach the Aggies for two seasons – that 5-7 1969-70 campaign and a 6-5-1 1970-71 season. Mark Stephenson would take over and his three years at the helm would be successful. The Aggies would win 31 of 39 dual meets and also make some serious headway in the MAC Championships, finishing as high as 2nd. But in 1974, Stephenson left and Delaware Valley College was again searching for a head coach. Once more they contacted Robert Marshall, who had actually left Dickinson and was selling cars. But he was ready to jump back into the fray.

"They called me and asked if I was still interested and I told them yes and that's what happened. I drove down, got the job and that was it."

Marshall was obviously familiar with the Del Val program and thought it was primed to take a big step.

"They had had winning seasons, but they were just floating along as far as I was concerned. They needed to have somebody come in there and just do the recruiting program. So when I got in there I just started doing that."

Marshall made recruiting the focal point of his wrestling program, relentlessly pursuing wrestlers he thought would be a perfect fit.

"I pushed myself every day to make phone calls and I think that's really what did it for me because a lot of coaches wouldn't do it. They would make a phone call every couple of weeks, or so. I would call almost every night, the kids that I was interested in. Just to let them know that I was interested in them."

Marshall would continue with the type of success that Stephenson had had. But he was also starting to build a long-term foundation for excellence that would lead to not just many more wins than losses, but also to team and individual success on a regional and national level that programs at the Division III level had rarely seen.

"I think it took like 4 or 5 years to work it out where we started to get really strong."

It was recruiting that was getting it done. Marshall was getting better wrestlers to call Doylestown home and then in the early 80s all those phone calls paid off in a watershed recruiting class coming to town.

"We kiddingly called them the 'Fab 5' because they really started the winning tradition there. After getting those five in the program, eventually people started seeing that Del Val was a pretty decent program and I started to get strong kids, like state qualifiers, interested."

The "Fab 5" included Marshall's son Troy, Bruce Stajnrajh, Tony Tarsi, Mark Sands and Tony Borrello. And while they are now looked at as the group that really helped take the program to new heights, Marshall says their overall success took him by surprise.

"Because actually none of those kids were state qualifiers. They were just good high school wrestlers that developed as the years went on. They were really the first group that we won a MAC (Middle Atlantic Conference) Championship with and then everybody said 'Wow, I guess Del Val really has the program going.'"

You never forget your first, and that initial MAC Title for the school came in 1982. It wasn't just the first championship in wrestling for the Aggies, it was their first overall, outright MAC title in any sport.

"It was unbelievable. It really was," Marshall remembers. "You would have thought we won a national title actually because the school had never had that happen before and for it to be the first and happen in wrestling. I mean it was great."

The "Fab 5" would continue to raise the bar of the program, winning every one of their 16 dual meets in '82-'83 and finishing second in the MAC Championships that season and the following one.

"Then they graduated, and everyone thought the program was going to go down," Marshall remembers, "but I was able to keep on recruiting pretty decent kids and it kept going at that point."

One of those "pretty decent kids" was a wrestler named Shaun Smith.

"He was a HS State Champ in PA and he was recruited heavily in Division I and he went to Lock Haven," Marshall recalls. "But in a Division I program, they pretty much own you and that's not the way

DELAWARE VALLEY COLLEGE ATHLETICS

Shaun Smith was a three-time National Champion at Delaware Valley College while losing just one of his 89 career matches.

he wanted to go. He was a workaholic as it was, so he left Lock Haven and went home and I found out that he was home and just started recruiting him and it took me like a year and a half to get him to come to Del Val. Eventually he came and he was very successful."

You could say that.

Wrestling at 142 pounds, Smith would become one of the most dominant wrestlers in the nation and the most decorated grappler in Aggie history. He would become the first individual National Champion at Delaware Valley College, actually turning that trick three times in 1985, 1986 and 1989. He would compete in 89 matches during his career. And lose once. It came in the 1987 National Finals. He is one of only six wrestlers in Division III history to capture at least three national titles.

Smith's first national championship actually holds a special place in Coach Marshall's heart.

"That was an unbelievable feeling. Because at that time they showed the NCAA Tournament on ESPN so we were on there, and I mean that's something that I'll never forget because it exposed the whole program to a bigger field. Having a kid win a national title, that's just a huge step."

Smith's third and final title in 1989 would be one piece of a very incredible puzzle for the Aggies that year. He was joined as a national champion by two other Delaware Valley College wrestlers, 158-pounder Mark Ambrose and 167-pounder Randy Worrell. It's the only time in school history they have had three national champs in one year.

"Worrell, because his bracket was so strong, we didn't think he would be able to win it. We thought he would be able to place, but we didn't think he would be able to win it," Marshall remembers. "When he won, we just started looking at each other — three national champs! It was just unbelievable. The thing that was disappointing was that we lost the national title by 6. The reason for that is that Ithaca had 9 people go to the tournament and we only had 4. And of course all 9 of theirs placed and the one kid that didn't place for us, all he had to do was win one match and we would have won that tournament. But we had 3 National Champions, so that was huge."

Marshall had now been at the helm of the Aggie program for some 15 years. If there had been any doubt that Doylestown was home to one of not just the region's, but the nation's, premier wrestling programs, 1989's three National Champions, plus the fact that his team won another MAC Championship and all 18 of its dual matches, erased them. That team also won the National Duals in January of

1989 and spent time ranked #1 in Division III.

It was more of the same to start the nineties. Incredibly intimidating won-loss records were joined by more MAC titles. Marshall's coaching staff was also joined by Smith, providing the present with an impressive link to its recent past.

In the fall of 1992, another special talent made his way to Doylestown after transferring from Rutgers. His name – Brandon Totten. "My father's an alum, so I was familiar with the area, familiar with the school and became familiar with the program through my father," Totten remembers.

"I originally went the Division I tract my freshman year in college and the school was too big. It was a state school and it just wasn't what I was looking for. And it took me going there a year to figure out that I needed to be at a smaller school like Delaware Valley in order to make the best of things."

"He was a hard worker. He wasn't the most talented wrestler but he was a hard worker and he was focused on winning a national title," Marshall says. "He actually did it the right way; he was more concerned about the end of the year than he was about winning matches throughout the year. He knew how to prepare himself for the National Tournament and, when he got to the National Tournament, he was ready."

Totten, a 158-pounder, who would win two National Championships in 1995 and 1996, says those quests started with the more modest, but still lofty goal of becoming an All-American, meaning a top-8 finish in his weight class.

"My junior year (1995) I think I took the 5th seed into the National Tournament," Totten remembers. "You know how upsets go, the #1 seed got knocked off by the #8 seed, the two seed lost to the 7 seed and I beat the four seed. So I find myself in the semifinals my junior year and I was an All-American. So at that point, talking to my family, my coaches, and my friends on the team, they were like 'You could really win this thing.' So I said well I'm here, I don't feel any different; I just feel a lot of relief because I am an All-American. And I may never get another chance to be in this position. So I reset my goal. I wanted to be the National Champ at the Tournament. And I was lucky enough for it to come true. It was my birthday that day. I went 2-0 (on the second day of the tournament) and I won the National Championship as a junior."

Totten would wrestle an incredible

DELAWARE VALLEY COLLEGE ATHLETICS

Aggies Head Coach Brandon Totten

60 matches his senior year on the way to defending his title.

"The second one is harder to win because the bulls-eye's on you, everybody is gunning for you. They are coming to scout you; they've got you on tape. They know you much better. The first year I was the fifth seed I wasn't supposed to win it but I did. It was definitely a tremendous feeling both years, but it was an even better feeling when I won the second one."

In the mid-90s, as Totten was winning his titles, there was a shift in the collegiate wrestling landscape, which gave the Aggie program another chance to shine, Coach Marshall explains.

"The NCAA went to regional championships and you had to place there to move on to the National Tournament."

Delaware Valley College Wrestling

All this change did was give the Aggies a chance to add a new banner to the wrestling room. With Totten leading the way, they would capture the NCAA East Regional title in both the 1994-95 and 1995-96 seasons.

"For us to win that, because you were in another group of schools, you really didn't know how you were going to do when you faced them; it was another level which I thought was great for the program."

Both those regional titles came after Del Val had already won MAC titles both years. So if you're counting at home, since Marshall took over, Delaware Valley College had now won eight MAC Championships.

As the nineties gave way to a new century, Coach Marshall started to look past his coaching days and contemplated retirement.

"When I turned 60 (in 2000), I thought when I turn 62 I'm going to retire and didn't think much more about that. Then I turned 61 and I thought, 'Well its time to hang 'em up.' For like two years it was on my mind, I had pretty much made up my mind when I turned 62 that I would retire."

The program had notched a 9th MAC title in 2000 and, as Marshall entered his final season as head coach, he hoped to go out on top. The Aggies went 9-5 in dual meets in 2001-02, which is a bit of a down year for this program, so they were by no means the favorites when the MAC Championships rolled around.

"None of the coaches, none of the people in the MAC thought we were going to win and I kept telling my athletic director 'if everything falls right, we can win this championship this year.'"

And sure enough, the plan came together.

"We got the seeds that we needed to get and of course the kids just wrestled their butts off and did a super job," Marshall says. "And some kids that shouldn't have won, won matches which made the difference. It was special, it really was. I still remember Shaun

DELAWARE VALLEY COLLEGE ATHLETICS

Jamall Johnson won a National Championship as a wrestler at Delaware Valley College.

(Smith) looking at me and he said, 'I don't believe it, I don't believe it,' whenever we finally got the points to put us over."

With that MAC Championship, the Robert Marshall era as head wrestling coach came to an end. It really was the type of run that legends are made of. During his 28 years at Del Val, Marshall would compile a dual meet mark of 363-67 and, of course, never have a losing season. The closest was a 10-10 year in 1979-80. The ten MAC Championships the program won would be complimented by its 12 second-place finishes. He would mentor 42 All-Americans and 83 MAC champions, and have four wrestlers win seven National Championships.

When you start talking about replacing a legacy like that, many times the best place to look is within. That is to say, someone who has an understanding of what it means to be a Del Val wrestler and an appreciation for what Marshall had built. Someone like two-time National Champion and the program's all-time leader in victories (122) - Brandon Totten.

"I didn't want the program going to some stranger coming in,"

Delaware Valley College Wrestling

Marshall recalls. "Brandon had a pretty good reputation for recruiting which was a major thing. He was able to recruit kids and transfer that too with his wrestling abilities because he was successful and the kids knew that so they respected him."

Totten left his post as head coach at Middlesex County College in New Jersey to come back and lead his alma mater at the age of 28.

"Talk about the pressure, you have a lot of doubters – 'Can he handle it? He was a good wrestler but does that make him a good coach?'" Totten says. "It was definitely something that I looked forward to myself but I needed to show everybody that I was capable of doing it. That first year Coach Marshall tutored me a lot over the phone. I kept him pretty close to me that year and I got through it. I like being here. It's a challenge, it's a great school and I enjoy the kids."

Those doubters would quickly be quieted, as the program did not miss a beat in Totten's first year, winning 17 of 20 dual meets and picking up the 11th MAC Championship in school history. Totten would be named the Division III Rookie Coach of the Year and MAC Coach of the Year for his trouble.

There would be no end in sight for Aggie dominance, and amid a new generation of great wrestlers came a transfer from Gloucester County College named Jamall Johnson.

"I didn't know much about the tradition. I just knew Coach Totten from when he coached against me a couple years beforehand when he coached at Middlesex," Johnson remembers.

Totten was able to recruit Johnson to come to Doylestown in 2004, and he says it didn't take long for him to realize he had joined a special program.

"After we had out first dual meet. In a lot of rooms you have a lot of good guys, a lot of guys with names and some wrestlers are what you call a 'practice hero.' They are able to do things in practice that they are not able to do in a match. So when we got to the first match and we kind of destroyed a team that probably shouldn't wrestle us it was like 'Wow, this team is pretty good.'"

And so was Johnson. Wrestling at 197, Johnson would go right to the head of the class during his two years at Del Val.

"My goal was to be an All-American, and then National Champ comes after that. You have to be an All-American first before you become a National Champ, so both years that was my goal just to be an All-American."

Johnson would become a two-time All-American but he fell just short of that National Championship his first year, losing in the finals. He would return to the finals in 2006, and he would cap his Aggie career with the 8th individual National Championship in school history.

"It's a great feeling. I still really don't grasp how much it meant sometimes, but it was a great experience. I'd love to be able to do it again."

Johnson's eligibility did expire after that National title, but he stayed on, like many Aggies, to spend some time as an assistant coach with the program.

The end of the decade has seen more excellence in Doylestown. Now competing in the NCAA Midwest Regionals, the Aggies won that title in 2007, 2008 and 2009. And in 2009, another National Champion would emerge in the 184 pound weight-class, as senior Mike Wilcox claimed the prize. In the process, he also became the first Aggie wrestler to be named the Most Outstanding Wrestler at the NCAA Division III Championships.

Needless to say, the Delaware Valley College wrestling program has become a national power. And while they compete at the Division III level, their dominance is not limited to this. For proof of that, check out the fact that the Aggies went 4-0 against Division I programs in dual meet action during the 2008-2009 season. Decades of excellence have, without question, created an aura around the program.

Delaware Valley College Wrestling

"My new assistant coach is Elliot Spence. He's a three-time All-American from Mt. St. Joe and they are in our (region)," Totten says. "He told me, 'You guys put a lot of fear in kids just with your name and all your rankings and your accolades.' A lot of times kids were beat on his team even before they stepped foot on the mat.' Having consecutive winning seasons over and over, it gets embedded into your opponents and their families and their coaches, and they realize they are going to have to have their A game just to try and beat us."

A lot of people have had a hand in building the Del Val dynasty and I think one of the best aspects of the program is how they have created a "family" atmosphere, with so many standout wrestlers coming back to coach or help the program. It really helps to cultivate the sense of pride that you can't help but notice whenever you talk to anyone associated with it. As for Robert Marshall, the true architect, it also provides bragging rights with brother Floyd – who was the last coach to have a losing season at the head of the Aggies.

"Oh yeah. I kid him about that. I bring it up all the time."

John Slaney

"Having coached Johnny and gotten to know Johnny, it was just a privilege to have him around for as long we did because he's a good person and obviously a great player."

– FORMER FLYERS AND PHANTOMS COACH JOHN STEVENS

There are some records that hit you how special they are right away. Then there are others that you need to think about for a minute and take in to appreciate how impressive they really are. I think the mark that John Slaney set on December 30th, 2005 falls into the latter category. On that night, the veteran Philadelphia Phantom became the AHL's all-time highest scoring defenseman. Not a bad line on a resume, especially when you consider the American Hockey League has been around since 1936.

To call Slaney a hockey "veteran" is probably an understatement. He was the Washington Capitals first-round pick and the 9th selection overall way back in 1990.

"For a kid coming out of (St. John's) Newfoundland, to play hockey was the one thing you wanted to go on and do and you always dream about wearing an NHL sweater," Slaney remembers.

After spending some time in the OHL as a teenager, Slaney would get his first taste of the NHL's top minor league, the American Hockey League, with the Baltimore Skipjacks. He would play six games with them during the 1991-92 season, and log his first six AHL points. He

PHILADELPHIA FLYERS

Slaney is congratulated by former Flyer great Ron Hextall after setting his AHL scoring record.

would spend the entire 1992-93 season in Baltimore and play very well, logging 66 points in 79 games and adding seven assists in seven playoff games. His performance here helped open the door for him to make his NHL debut the following season. He would wear the Washington Capitals sweater during the 1993-94 campaign, and notch his first NHL goal. That special moment would occur at the Spectrum against the Flyers, and it would not be the first time that he would have a fond memory at "America's Showplace".

"It was in the second period," Slaney remembers. "Basically, the puck came around the boards and I just took it and looked up. I was hoping to hit the guy in the slot, and when I shot the puck it went straight through the goalie's legs and into the net."

Slaney would go on to play 47 games with Washington, but also 29 games with Portland of the AHL. Getting to the NHL is one thing, but staying there may be even tougher. For the next several years, Slaney would bounce around, making stops in the NHL with teams like Los Angeles, Colorado, Phoenix and Nashville, while also skating in the IHL and of course logging more time in the AHL. But he never found a place to really set up shop and call home.

"It was definitely frustrating because it's part of the game that you have to stay at a high quality of play all the time," Slaney says. "You have to be at your best no matter what you are doing. In my case, it didn't help me that I got hurt so many times over the years. That kind of hurts when you're out 3, 4 or even 6 weeks when you are injured. Especially when you are on a team having guys up and down and not winning a lot of games and new guys are coming in and playing, so it was kind of tough that way. You don't know when you are young the mental part of the game, that you have to stay focused at all times and that was the eye opener for me when I got a little older."

Slaney would spend the 1999-2000 season with the Penguins organization and, as had become the drill for his career, he would get a taste of the NHL – skating with Pittsburgh for 29 games – but most of his season was spent in the minors with the AHL's Wilkes-Barre Penguins. Slaney would have an outstanding AHL campaign, logging 60 points in just 49 games.

The following season he started in Wilkes-Barre once again, but then during the AHL All-Star break in January he was traded to the Flyers organization in a deal that brought defenseman Kevin Stevens to Pittsburgh. And really for the first time, Slaney would find a hockey home in Philadelphia. While he would only play a handful of games with the Flyers over seven seasons with the organization, he would become one of the most popular players in the AHL Phantoms' history.

"They took care of me. I mean it was a great organization, a first class organization. They want the best for Philadelphia and for the Flyers organization and I think they do it the right way."

Slaney also piled up the points as a Phantom and gained a reputation as one the league's best blueliners. He would win the Eddie Shore Award, given to the AHL's top defenseman, following the 2000-01 and 2001-02 seasons. He also became a respected veteran in the Phantoms locker room.

"He took care and made sure all the younger guys kind of knew what their role was and knew what they were doing and helped out where he could," says former Phantom forward and Philadelphia native, Tony Voce.

"We became really good friends," Voce says. "I think he laughed at me, at some of the things I would do. I was kind of a character and he sat next to me in the locker room and just laughed at my stories and we became good friends and still today are good friends."

2005 would turn into quite a calendar year for Slaney. First, he would help the Phantoms win a Calder Cup that June, as they rolled through the playoffs, eventually sweeping Chicago in the finals.

"He was a real key member and there were a lot of NHL players on that Calder Cup team, but he was a real key member and contributor on that team," recalls former Phantoms and Flyers Coach John Stevens. "He was great. I can honestly say we would have been in trouble without him."

Then, as the Phantoms attempted to defend their title, word started to emerge that Slaney was approaching an impressive mark — the AHL record for most career points by a defenseman. At the time, a gentleman named Steve Kraftcheck, who played for several AHL teams in the 50s and 60s, and also logged NHL time with Boston, the Rangers and Toronto, held the record. Kraftcheck was also a 2008 inductee into the AHL Hall of Fame.

"My sister just happened to go on the Internet one night and noticed that I was coming close to a record," Slaney remembers. "At the time I don't think we were winning very many games and I remember saying to her that I just want to win a game here because we are losing so many. My sister told me and then I remember (Phantoms PR man Mike Thornton) coming up to me one night after a loss and saying, 'You aren't very far from it' and I remember saying the same thing to him."

Regardless of the circumstances, Slaney was approaching immortality and he was tied with Kraftcheck at 453 points heading into the December 30th, 2005 game at the Spectrum against Bridgeport.

"I told him before the game that I'm going to score the goal to break the record for you and he was like, 'Yeah, right,'" Voce remembers.

The Phantoms were trailing 2-0 in the third period when they went on the power play. One of the reasons Slaney has played hockey for some two decades is his ability to play the blue line with the man advantage, so if the historic point were going to come - this was a good bet as to when. Slaney, however, was more focused on getting the Phantoms back in the game.

"At the time we needed to score a goal."

For his part, Voce was ready to make good on his pregame prediction.

"He got the puck at the point and I kind of went and stood at the side of the net because there was a lot of traffic in front. I know he (Slaney) is a smart guy, so he looks to kind of put it to the side and hope that someone will be there to tap it in. So I kind of got to the right side of the net and he wound up and took a slap shot. (Josh Gratton) deflected it on the way in and I was just standing there on the back door and all I had to do was tap it in. I had an open net; it was already behind the goalie and everything. So I just tapped it in. I grabbed the puck right away to make sure that he had it and gave it to the guys on the bench."

"He (Voce) is like, 'You did it, you did it!' And I'm like, 'Did what?' 'You got the point, you broke the record!' I'm like, 'Yeah, I did.' I was kind of surprised but at the same time, I was happy I did it," Slaney remembers.

That would be the only highlight that night for the Phantoms, as they would lose 4-1. But it was a moment that would live in AHL history. However, after the game, Voce says Slaney didn't really focus on it.

"I think it was definitely brought up in the locker room by guys, congratulations were said to him. But for him I don't think he said anything. He thanked everybody and that was about it."

"I don't really realize it until you sit down and think about it or talk about it," Slaney says. "You always want them to remember how you played and what kind of player you were. As long as people think about it and realize what you did for the league and how you did it more than anything else. It's something that my son now realizes; he's getting older, and he realizes what happened and he's playing hockey so he is pretty excited for that too."

Slaney would finish the 2005-06 season with 50 points in 79 games for the Phantoms. He would spend one more season in Philadelphia, tallying 33 points in 50 games during the 2006-07 campaign.

"I think Johnny is a really proud guy and he wanted to be a good player so you want to be counted on, you want to play key situations," remembers Stevens. "He always came out and played hard every night and wanted to make a difference. He had great vision, great passer, great one timer, so he's an extremely smart player. But I think he was a little underrated how good he was defensively because I know when we were in the playoffs, we really counted on him at the end of games. Game on the line - he's a guy we want on the ice. He had a tremendous AHL career."

Since leaving Philadelphia, Slaney has been playing in Germany. As it stands, to become the all-time highest scoring defenseman in AHL history now requires 520 points. One more than Slaney's career total. So how does he look at his career? He's obviously one of the greatest defensemen in the history of the AHL, but his longevity at that level means, for whatever reason, he was never able to establish himself in the NHL.

"You'll always be happy with what you did, but at the same time your goal was to play in the National Hockey League as long as you can. Definitely the frustration sets in because certain things you thought you did right, they thought you did wrong. It's never an even street when you think about it," Slaney says. "You can get mad about it for so long, but you have to move on and you have to put the past in the past. The 'shoulda, coulda, wouldas' will always be there. At the same time, you can never be disappointed because only so many players can play this game for so long. For me, playing for 19 years, I'm pretty happy to still be playing hockey."

Jeff Reese

"I know one of my defensemen was mad at me. I think it was Greg Smyth, because I passed him in scoring, so he was a little ticked off."

– GOALTENDER JEFF REESE
ON HIS RECORD SETTING NIGHT

I remember watching the Flyers game on December 8th, 1987 when Ron Hextall became the first goalie to actually shoot and score a goal in a NHL game. The Islanders' Billy Smith had been credited with a goal in 1979, but he was simply the last Islander to touch an errant puck. Hextall actually took aim at an empty net and connected. It was a very cool moment, one of those where you took that half second double-take wondering if you just saw what you thought you saw. But as special as that was, I think what current Flyers goaltending coach Jeff Reese pulled off on February 10th, 1993 is even more unbelievable. While between the pipes for the Calgary Flames that night, he became the first and only goalie in NHL history to tally three assists in a single game.

On that February night, Reese's Flames were hosting San Jose in what looked to be a pretty non-descript midseason NHL game. Calgary was chasing Vancouver for first place in the Smythe Division, while the Sharks were, frankly, awful.

"San Jose was an expansion team (1992-93 was their second year of existence) and we had a very good team in Calgary. We had (Gary) Roberts, (Joe) Nieuwendyk, (Al) MacInnis, and (Gary) Suter. We had (Theo) Fleury," Reese remembers.

Jeff Reese played goalie for five teams (pictured with Tampa Bay) during his 11 NHL seasons.

The Sharks had just six wins in 54 games coming into this one, on their way to an NHL-record 71-loss season. It was a bit surprising when they scored first, as Johan Garpenlov beat Reese on the power-play about three minutes in to give San Jose a 1-0 lead. However, that would be the end of the Shark highlights for the evening.

Calgary would tie it at the 12:26 mark on a Suter goal and then take the lead for good, all of 17 seconds later when Robert Reichel lit the lamp. This second goal would be the first one for which Reese would be credited an assist. The Flames would go on to score two more in the period and head into the first intermission up 4-1.

Reese struck again more than midway through the second period, getting assist number two on the Flames' fifth goal, which was scored by Gary Roberts. Calgary would get two more that period and led

7-1 after 40 minutes of hockey. The third period saw this game go from blowout to absurdity. The Flames scored three goals in the first minute of the stanza, expanding their lead to 10-1. Then, at the 9:41 mark, history was made. Goal #11 was scored by Reichel, his second of the game, with the assists going to Al MacInnis and, you guessed it, Jeff Reese, his third of the game.

"To be quite honest with you, after the game nobody really had any idea it was a record," Reese remembers.

Calgary would go on to light the lamp two more times, putting the finishing touches on a 13-1 laugher. Reese says, despite the final score, his first priority of net minding wasn't quite as easy as you would think.

"You know what? The game ended up 13-1, but I actually remember playing not too bad a game. I had to make a few saves in the game so I felt pretty good."

Reese would make 26 of those saves between the pipes, but obviously it was his offensive prowess that night that has endured, although he says this record was by no means by design.

"I know one thing. It wasn't like I was throwing pucks up the middle on the guys' tape up at center ice or anything like that. It was just maybe dishing it off to a defenseman and then we went down and scored. The poor goalies down the other end, everything seemed to go in that night."

Those poor goalies were Arturs Irbe and Jeff Hackett for San Jose. How bad did it get for them? Irbe started and was pulled after the first period. Hackett replaced him, but he only stopped 9 of the 15 shots he faced. So San Jose actually put Irbe back in a few minutes into the third period to absorb the rest of the beating. Despite scoring 13 goals, the Flames had only 36 shots.

While he stands alone at the top of a goaltender scoring record, Reese would tally only five other assists in the other 173 regular season games of his career over portions of 11 seasons and says he never really considered handling the puck a real strength of his game.

"No. I wasn't one of the better guys, obviously, but it is something that once I turned pro I really started to work on, especially in the minors and I feel it's a big part of the game. I feel it can help out there. I really believe it's something that is a tremendous asset to have. But it was more of a fluke that night. I would never compare myself to a (Martin) Brodeur or a Hextall or anybody like that. It was just more of a fluky thing."

To give some perspective on this record and just how incredible it really is — Hextall was considered one of, if not the best, stickhandler when it came to goaltenders. He scored the goal mentioned earlier and also struck for another in a playoff game later in his career. But his career high for points in a season was 8 in 1988-89. 8 points in 64 games. Reese had three in one game. But he still isn't expecting to sit at the top of that list alone forever.

"I think it will at least be tied someday, it will be broken. Especially now. You know the kids, not only are they learning to stop the puck a little differently than when I was growing up, but they are also learning to handle the puck. It's such a good dimension to have but I think somebody will break it someday. But it's nice to have."

Reese was hired as the Flyers' goaltending coach in the summer of 2009 and he says the job is a dream come true. Even though he was raised in Canada, he grew up a die-hard Flyers fan or, more specifically, a fan of legendary Flyers goaltender Bernie Parent.

"That's kind of how I got hooked, not just on the Flyers, but goaltending. I played a lot like Bernie growing up. I stood up on everything. The game's evolved and changed, but that's how I played. It really is a dream come true and that's coming straight from the heart. Bernie Parent was my guy and now I'm good friends with Bobby 'The Chief' Taylor, who actually backed up Bernie, and it's a special thing for me. I really can't emphasize enough how excited I am to be here. And it sure would be nice to win a championship here, that's for sure."

Mike Washington

"I'd be lying if I said I didn't pay some sort of attention to it. But I like winning a lot more than setting records. I like team achievements more than I do individual ones."

– MIKE WASHINGTON ON HIS NUMEROUS RECEIVING RECORDS

The average college football season is 11, maybe 12 games. I think that most coaches would be pretty happy if, over the course of a season, they could get five touchdowns from a starting wide receiver. That's about a score every other game, which is solid production. Now consider getting five touchdowns in ONE game. That's off the chart. Especially if it turns out it's the player's first ever college football game as a redshirt freshman! Ladies and gentlemen, I'd like to introduce you to West Chester legend Mike Washington.

The Golden Rams opened the 2005 season against Clarion. Head Coach Bill Zwaan had won everywhere he'd been, and West Chester was no exception, so expectations were high heading into the campaign. Offensively, the Golden Rams had a wonderful returning wide receiver in Brandon Simmons. But they also had a youngster who had been creating a lot of buzz since arriving from Frankford High School.

Washington was not heavily recruited as he didn't get the ball much at Frankford. He says Division I-AA schools James Madison and Villanova dipped their toes in the water with him, but Division II

Mike Washington caught five touchdown passes in his first collegiate game as a redshirt freshman.

West Chester was the only school that really pushed to bring him on board. Coach Zwaan says it did not take long for him and his staff to realize they had something special.

"The time it really hit us was in the All-Star (Philadelphia Daily News City) Game and in fact, I was watching the game on TV and somebody called me and said, 'Hey, is that kid going to West Chester?' because he made couple of unbelievable catches. And we had been hearing from the all-star practices how good he looked."

Washington actually arrived on the scene in 2004, but took a redshirt the first year since the Golden Rams already had two outstanding receivers in Simmons and Cory DeForrest. But he made his presence known to players like then Rams back-up quarterback Bill Zwaan Jr.

"I threw the ball over the middle once when we were practicing together on the scout team against our first team defense," Zwaan Jr. remembers. "He jumped up and made this one-handed catch and everybody, even the older guys turned and went 'Oh, ok.'"

Washington would continue to wow teammates and coaches on an almost daily basis throughout the season, and his incredible ability led Zwaan to actually consider the extraordinary step of taking him out of that redshirt as the season intensified.

"We were going towards the playoffs and we had a really good team. It was probably, maybe, the 9th or 10th game of the season. We sat down as an offensive staff and said, 'He's that good that if we get to the playoffs,' like we were figuring we were going to, 'he might be the difference in us winning that game that could take us to the National Championship.'"

Because of the presence of Simmons and DeForest, Zwaan says that, despite the temptation, they decided making a move at that point wasn't fair to Washington. So Washington entered the 2005 season with four full years of eligibility remaining.

Washington started at wide receiver that first game against Clarion.

"We just kept thinking, we had Brandon Simmons back who had a great year the year before," Zwann says, "and I thought 'this is going to be a nice complementary player to Brandon.'"

It took all of three plays for Washington to show he would be more than a complement.

His FIRST score was a 64-yard touchdown catch and run.

"The coaches knew they were going to be keying on him (Simmons) and leave the middle of the field pretty much open. That's exactly what happened and I caught the ball and just ran with it. I was wide open."

Then a few minutes later, on West Chester's next offensive play, Washington would score on a 67-yard bomb. Next up, junior quarterback Matt Burdalski found Washington for a 17-yard touchdown. And then the first quarter ended. With 15 minutes of college football game experience in his pocket, Washington had caught three balls and turned them all into touchdowns. Not bad. Needless to say, Clarion had taken notice.

"They were as surprised as I was," Washington remembers. "They were talking to me on the field and they were like, 'Who are you? What year are you?' Really everybody thought I was a senior until I told them I was a freshman."

He would score touchdowns four and five in the third quarter, from 24 and 31 yards out. The five touchdown catches set a West Chester school record. His 242 receiving yards that day was the third best single game performance in school history. It also helped the Golden Rams to an easy 43-14 win in front of some 5,200 fans at John A. Farrell Stadium. Obviously, they were just as impressed as Coach Zwaan was.

"As the game was wearing on, we (the coaches) were saying stuff to each other like, ' Boy we got something here; this kid is something special.' Then I think it was after the game, we got a chance to sit around and talk about it and just said, 'Now we have to concentrate on getting him the ball and figure out what to do with him because he's that good.'"

"I think after the game everybody was kind of like, 'Hey, look at the freshman – he's big time,'" remembers Zwaan Jr. "He was all smiles after the game and that was really his coming out party and everybody started talking about 'who is Mike Washington' and that's when it started."

For his part, Washington says the significance of his debut wasn't lost on him.

"It really didn't hit me until after the game. I think I felt I could be some type of playmaker or have a good impact on the game with our offense, but it really didn't hit me like that until after the game was over and I looked back and was like, 'Wow - I just had five touchdowns.'"

The redshirt freshman quickly turned into the focal point of the West Chester offensive attack and his first season ended with 47 catches for 1,185 yards and 15 touchdowns.

Heading into his sophomore season, Washington would not have the benefit of an accomplished receiver like Brandon Simmons on the other side of the field. And, according to Zwaan, opponents worked hard to eliminate the Golden Rams star from the game plan.

"There were games where people just did everything they could physically try to beat him up, double team him, try to sneak another guy on top of him - and it worked to a certain extent. But the nice thing about our offense that has made us successful is we have always been able to go to other people when somebody was shut down. So if somebody really spent a lot of time trying to shut Mike down - we let them - and then we would go to somebody else."

Despite all of the attention, Washington still put together a wonderful sophomore campaign, catching 55 balls for 1,170 yards and 16 more touchdowns. When asked if there was a play that really stood out during his career, it was one of those sophomore season scores that Washington points to because of its significance beyond the scoreboard.

It was the last game of the regular season and the Golden Rams were battling Slippery Rock on the road and needed a win to really cement their playoff hopes. Time was winding down in the first half and West Chester trailed 10-7. An impressive drive had stalled at the Slippery Rock 15 and the Golden Rams were facing 4th down.

"Coach Zwaan has the field goal team on the field. And his son Bill (Zwaan Jr.) had talked him into just throwing me a fade. Coach called his last timeout of the half and we went out there and ran it and scored a touchdown."

"I just said 'screw this - let's throw a fade to Mike.'" the younger Zwaan remembers, "And he (Coach Zwaan) was like 'alright let's do it' and we ran a fade to Mike which was a big touchdown."

"It just made me feel good – I mean I was still pretty young at that point," Washington remembers. "It made me feel good to know that the coach had enough confidence in me to take the field goal team off and throw me the ball."

West Chester would go on to win at Slippery Rock for the first time since FDR was in office and make the playoffs. They would advance to the second round before being eliminated in heartbreaking fashion by Bloomsburg when a potential game-winning field goal was partially blocked with a minute to play. This would prove to be the hump the Golden Rams could never get over during Washington's tenure. They would make the playoffs in each of his four years and get to the second round twice, but no further.

That Slippery Rock moment was just one in a long list of special ones for Zwaan Jr, who loved having a receiver – and friend – like Washington.

"Through the years we ended up just staying and living on campus during the summer. And working together every day. We would throw and lift together. So we knew each other inside and out on the field and what we had going to do. I would come to the line of scrimmage and Mike would look at me. If he had a kid on him, he would give me a smirk like 'I'm going to beat this kid.' And I was like, 'Okay, I know where I'm going.' And if I ever got in trouble and I was running around back there – even if he had two, three guys on him - it didn't matter. You threw it up in the air because he was going to go get it."

Washington's junior season was another 12 game highlight reel. During his 49 catch, 1,160 yard, 12 touchdown campaign, he would become the school's all-time leader in receiving yards in a week #9 win over St. Joseph's (Ind). He would also notch a four-touchdown day in a September win over Bloomsburg. That game was yet another example of how Washington was a threat to score from anywhere on the field at any time. He only touched the ball seven times, but turned three of his four catches into six points, including a 77-yarder. He also ran for a 22-yard touchdown on one of his three carries. This leads us to examine what may be the most remarkable aspect of Washington's statistical career. He found the end zone 27% of the time he caught the ball. 58 touchdowns on 215 catches. To put it in perspective, while at Marshall, Randy Moss scored 32% of the time he caught the ball. Mississippi Valley State's Jerry Rice scored on 17% of his catches and Keyshawn Johnson, the last receiver to be taken #1 in the NFL draft out of USC, turned 11% of his 168 collegiate catches into six points. Are these fair comparisons? Who knows, but I think it's cool. And Coach Zwaan says the percentage of Washington's plays that came in the clutch was even higher.

"When we had to go to him in crucial situations - and that's really the thing - you know, two minute drills, end of the half, who are we going to? Everybody in the stands knows who we are going to and we hit him and he scores! That's the amazing thing. In the most crucial situations, when people knew where we were going with the football, he would come through for us. He was unstoppable and I think his level - he knew when his level had to go up - big games, big times in games, and his level went up."

Washington entered his final season at West Chester with the chance to just lay waste not only to more West Chester, but also Pennsylvania State Athletic Conference, and even NCAA, records. You can surmise that he did not disappoint. Washington caught a career-high 64 balls in 2008, for 1,200 yards and 15 touchdowns. He also added his second career score on the ground. Every week, Washington had the good people in the West Chester Sports Information Department (aka SID James Zuhlke) reaching for the record book.

Washington would become the Golden Rams' all-time leader in touchdown catches in a win over Kutztown. He would catch five balls for 155 yards and two touchdowns in the FIRST half against Lock Haven. When he passed the 1,000 yard mark, he became just the third player in the history of college football, at any level, to do that in each of his four seasons. His excellence catapulted the Golden Rams back to the playoffs where they would win in the opening round over Southern Connecticut 52-32. This earned them the right to match up with PSAC foe Bloomsburg.

"On the bus ride up to Bloomsburg it was on my mind the whole time - this could be the last game of my career - and I just wanted to go out there and leave everything on the field if it was my last game, and I think I did that."

It was a back and forth contest all afternoon at Bloom, but the Golden Rams never led. Washington did all he could, catching 6 balls for 103 yards. His final catch was an 18-yard touchdown strike from Joe Wright that made it a 28-21 game with just under two minutes to play. But West Chester would not see the ball again.

"I realized that that was my last game when they got that first down to seal the victory and it hit me then - my college career is over."

So Washington's college career, which started with a touchdown on his first catch as a redshirt freshman, fittingly ended with a touchdown catch on his last play. In between, he would put together a career that saw him named first-team all-PSAC four times. As a senior, he was named a first team Division II All-American and was a finalist for the Harlon Hill trophy, the Division II Heisman Trophy. He played in the Cactus Bowl down in Texas, the Division II All-Star Game. He is third all-time in Division II and sixth across ALL divisions of college football with 4,715 receiving yards and 58 touchdown catches. He caught a ball in every one of the 50 games he played as a collegian, setting a NCAA Division II record. All totaled, he ended his career with 12 records on the school, conference and national level under his belt.

Washington was a complete football player. He wasn't one of those stereotypical pass catchers who wouldn't get his nose dirty. He would block.

"The thing I always talked about is his blocking. That's what made him such a well-rounded player. That's what our players all liked about him so much," Coach Zwaan says. "In our offense, our receivers have to block, especially the position he plays. And he loved blocking. And our kids saw him work hard at it, love doing it, never give up on a block, and I think that made our guys look at him a lot differently."

"He was one of the most physical wide receivers I have ever seen," recalls Zwaan Jr. "He would block anybody. He would come down and block defensive ends and linebackers. He was so tough, he was such a good football player - not just a great wide receiver - he was such a good football player."

Washington says the seeds for his blocking prowess were planted during his days at Frankford High.

"That's all we did. Blocking and tackling. Every day we hit a two-man sled. If we didn't do it right we were doing it over and over again. So that's where it came from."

Now we have the 6th all-time receiver in college football, who is also a beast when he doesn't have the ball. When the college season was over, it was time for the NFL scouts to move in. Believe it or not, despite what you've learned the last few pages, Washington garnered

WEST CHESTER ATHLETICS

Mike Washington caught 58 touchdown passes during his West Chester career.

next to no interest from the NFL - not getting drafted nor signing on as a rookie free agent.

"I don't know if they were scared away by my size (listed at 6-0, 190 lbs), speed, I don't know," Washington admits. "I have no clue how they were looking at me. I knew coming into my senior season that it was a long shot that I would make it, even make it to a NFL camp. I mean it disappointed me a little but life must go on."

Washington takes it all in stride.

"I haven't closed the chapter on football at all. If the opportunity presents itself, then I would try to jump back into it. But if I don't get another chance to play football then I'm satisfied with what I've accomplished."

Mike Washington

The man who spent a lot of time throwing Washington the football still doesn't get why his phone never rang.

"Mike had everything and that's what kind of throws me off that he didn't get a shot," Zwaan Jr says. "He at least deserved a shot because he was such a great football player."

If his college coach were making the call, you can believe Washington would be playing somewhere.

"I was watching the I-AA National Championship game and they threw Jerry Rice on and talked about his records and were showing highlights of him," Zwaan says. "And I sat back and I was like 'Mike passed him. Jerry Rice!!!' And then it kind of really hit me that Mike is one of the greatest receivers, statistically, in the history of college football. But to us he's just Mike and that's the way he always was. He didn't push that stardom on anyone; he just was Mike. I think that's part of the reason that it kind of shocks you when you sit back and think about it. He just did it day in and day out, game in and game out, and you didn't really realize his greatness until he put it all together and put it down on paper and you say, 'Boy, one of the greatest ever.'"

Ray Ventrone (#28) was an all-conference defensive back at Villanova.

Ray Ventrone

"He is really the epitome of what a Villanova football player is. He has a good mind, he's mentally disciplined, he's a very good football player and he's a great person."

– VILLANOVA FOOTBALL COACH ANDY TALLEY

Some of my favorite groups of stories every year comes from NFL prospects as they prepare/wait for the draft and the follow-ups after they were drafted or signed on as rookie free agents. There is a palpable excitement as guys get the chance to realize a dream they have worked toward for years. The rookie free agent route, however, is a difficult one. While some teams – the Eagles being an excellent example – more than give rookie free agents a chance to open their eyes, in many cases, these guys are simply brought into camp as a body with no one having any intention of them making the team. Regardless of the situation, it's a tough road to hoe, which makes you appreciate the tenacity, patience and hard work of former Villanova safety Ray Ventrone.

Ventrone hails from the Pittsburgh area and was a standout athlete at Chartiers Valley High School in Bridgeville, PA. In addition to making a name for himself on the gridiron, Ventrone set three track and field records in the long jump, triple jump and 100M. However, it was football that Ventrone decided to pursue at the next level and he chose Villanova over schools like Youngstown State, Wofford, and William and Mary.

"The coaching staff, the players, it was tight knit, like family. And I wanted to be a part of it. I was actually supposed to visit William and Mary the next week and I cancelled my visit. Didn't even take my visit there."

Ventrone arrived on the Main Line in 2001 and quickly became a stalwart in the Wildcat defensive backfield, impressing longtime Wildcat head coach Andy Talley.

"He started to hit people right off the bat. I called him a heat-seeking missile."

As a junior, he earned All-Atlantic 10 First Team honors as a safety and also drew constant praise for standout work on the Wildcat special teams. In fact, Ventrone's ability to hit became the stuff of legends on the Mainline, according to Coach Talley.

"Towards the end of his career here, I wouldn't let him hit any of our players (in practice). He hit (a wide receiver) coming across the middle one time and knocked him cold. He woke up and said, 'Coach, keep that boy away from me. I don't want to see him again.' He was dangerous."

Needless to say, Ventrone and the Wildcats had high hopes heading into his senior year in 2004. The team was highly regarded and Ventrone had caught the attention of NFL scouts. However, things went off the rails in week 4 during a 16-13 win over cross-town rival Penn. Ventrone fractured his fibula and tore the deltoid ligament in his right foot. His season and college career came to an abrupt halt.

"It was tough and I don't think it really hit me until a week or two after I had been injured and I actually watched my teammates play without me," Ventrone says. "It was tough on me because I know how much the defense relied on me to be their leader and I wasn't able to be on the field."

How much did that defense rely on Ventrone? In the four games before he was injured, including the Penn win, the Wildcats allowed 15 points a game and went 3-1. In the seven games after he got hurt, they allowed more than 28 a game and went 3-4.

"He was the backbone of that defense," Coach Talley remembers. "It was difficult to lose him like that early in the season. We missed a real leader and a real tough guy. It was a tough loss for us."

Ventrone remained in a cast until early December, but he was able to shake off the disappointment of the injury even before that, as he worked his upper body and left leg, now turning his attention to what may lie ahead.

"I think I had the mindset about midway through the season that I couldn't feel bad for myself. I know I have an opportunity to play at the next level if I work hard. And that's when I really started to put it into gear."

Ventrone credits personal trainer Steve Saunders, who has worked with a host of NFL players, for getting him on track to be ready to show his wares for coaches and scouts as Draft Day 2005 arrived.

"Once I was healthy, I really was motivated to show everyone I could play again. In the 3 months leading up (to the draft), I trained my butt off. I had two classes at the time. And I went to class Tuesday and Thursday and then I would stay at Steve's house the remainder of the weekend and we would train. So he really got me ready. Rehabbed me. And it worked out well. I got real strong and had a good diet. I got real lean. And I really did run well at my pro day whenever it came time."

Coach Talley had confidence that Ventrone had pro potential.

"He was a sleeper that had a lot of good tape on him, and you sold him as having special teams potential because of his speed and his physicality. And he was a guy you hoped a team would take into camp because you knew that once he got into camp they would like what they saw."

Ventrone's phone started ringing as the second day of the draft wound down. There was some talk of New England making him "Mr. Irrelevant" and taking him with the 255th and final pick of the draft. However, they instead choose TE Andy Stokes out of William Penn University, which, as I'm sure you guessed immediately, is in Oskaloosa, Iowa. Don't worry. I had to look it up too.

However, while the Patriots drafted Stokes (who never played a down in the NFL), they didn't waste any time signing Ventrone as a rookie free agent.

"It was (now Cleveland Browns Head Coach) Eric Mangini who called me. He was the defensive backs' coach at the time and he said, 'Ray, we want to sign you as a free agent.' I was excited that I got a call to be signed by them. Even prior to the draft, my agent and I had discussed that going to New England would probably be my best opportunity."

Ventrone now had the chance to play pro football. As I mentioned earlier, the life of a rookie free agent is a tough one. But Ventrone says that he was ready for that first training camp - at least physically.

"The biggest transition is obviously the mental aspect. It's a lot more complex with the schemes and the calls and the playbook is a lot bigger. (It's) more complex overall from a mental standpoint. You know, from the physical standpoint I was just as fast and as strong as anyone on the field. The toughest adjustment for me was the mental aspect and obviously the game is a lot faster than the college game. It's like going from high school to college with the speed, and then from college to the NFL is even a bigger jump."

Ventrone impressed in that first training camp in 2005, but not enough to make the active roster. The Patriots, however, brought him on board their practice squad. And while many fans tend to dismiss the practice squad experience, Ventrone says it was invaluable.

"It really was a huge honor, especially not playing at all the season before. I think that it was a good year to bring me along after being out of football the whole season and I thought that that was a pretty good option as far as easing me in and bringing me along."

He says that life on the practice squad really isn't much different

Ray Ventrone makes his presence known against rival Delaware.

VILLANOVA MEDIA RELATIONS

than life on the active roster. In some cases, you actually have to do more. With the Patriots, Ventrone says practice squad players are required to lift four days a week, as opposed to the three days for active players.

"We attend every meeting, every practice. The only thing we really don't do is travel to away games and play on Sundays."

The season on the practice squad also let Ventrone display a versatility that would serve him well down the road. During the week, he would help the first team get a feel for what the Patriots' opponents were going to do that game by mimicking the opposition's players and tendencies. And because of his athleticism, he was doing it from many more positions then just his native safety.

"I basically played everything on offense except the line position. I played linebacker. One week I actually was at defensive end. Whenever we played Indianapolis, that week I was (Colts All-Pro pass rusher) Dwight Freeney in practice. I've emulated everybody from Dwight Freeney to Troy Polamalu to Brian Westbrook."

Ventrone chalked up an entire season on the practice squad and in the spring of 2006, New England sent him to play in the now-defunct NFL Europa, which served as a developmental league for the NFL until it was disbanded. He suited up for the Cologne Centurions in Germany and, for the first time since his senior year in college, got back into the weekly grind of a football season. He played well, finishing fourth on the team in tackles and he led the league with four forced fumbles. A little more than halfway through the season, however, the injury bug bit him once again. This time it was a shoulder. He played through the pain for the final few games. It wasn't until he returned stateside that he learned the injury was more serious than the bruise it was first diagnosed as. He had a torn labrum. He missed the entire 2006 NFL campaign.

The injury cost him more than just the season because in February, New England released him.

"I kind of saw it coming," Ventrone says. "I hadn't really played an NFL season and I was injured again. So I felt like there's a chance that they might keep me. But there's a pretty good chance that they won't."

However, Ventrone's unemployment would last only about a week as the Patriots' AFC East rivals, the New York Jets, came calling. Eric Mangini, the coach who called Ventrone to tell him he was being signed by the Pats as a rookie free agent, was now the top man in the

Big Apple. His time with the Jets, however, would prove a bit frustrating.

"I thought I played really well in the preseason with the Jets. I led the team in special teams tackles. I made a lot of plays in camp at safety and I thought I had done enough to earn a spot on the active roster. Unfortunately, I didn't."

The Jets did put Ventrone on their practice squad, but that was short-lived and in mid-September of 2007, New York let him go. Once again, Ventrone was not out of work for long.

"After I was released from the Jets, my agent told me that the Patriots wanted to sign me to the practice squad. It was a blessing in disguise. I couldn't have asked for a better situation. If I had to do it all over again, I wouldn't have changed anything."

So Ventrone headed back up to New England and stepped right back into his Patriots routine for the next couple of months, by opening eyes doing anything and everything on the practice squad. But despite all the hard work, the Villanova product still had yet to suit up for a regular season NFL game. That would all change on November 4th, 2007.

It was Week 9 in the NFL and the Patriots were heading out on the road to face Indianapolis. The Pats had lost to the Colts in Indy in the AFC Championship Game, 38-34, the season before. So, this rematch was highly anticipated even before the season started. Then it turned out that both teams were undefeated heading into the game, New England 8-0 with the Colts 7-0. In fact, this would be the first meeting in NFL history between two teams with records of 7-0 or better. The eyes of the NFL, really the entire sporting world, were descending upon the RCA Dome that afternoon. It was under these circumstances that Ray Ventrone would finally make his NFL debut.

"I can't even describe the feeling, whenever I walked into that stadium. Those fans were just going crazy. It really was electric. It was so loud I couldn't even hear myself talk."

Ventrone would see game action on special teams for the Patriots, who trailed this one 20-10 midway through the fourth quarter before Tom Brady threw two touchdown passes in the final eight minutes to give New England a 24-20 victory.

"My buddy was in law school at the time in Michigan State, Mark Fiorilli, and he drove all the way down to Indianapolis to see me play. It was pretty cool. I saw him up in the stands and it was just exciting to have someone at the game, my first game, and it was great. It really was."

Ventrone would be on the active roster for two more games that regular season, but only suit up for one of them. But once again, it was a nice notch to have on his belt. He played in the regular season finale against the New York Giants, the game the Patriots won to finish with an undefeated regular season at 16-0.

The Pats, obviously, had a first round bye in the playoffs and Ventrone wasn't active for the divisional playoff win against the Jaguars. He did, however, play special teams in the AFC Championship win over San Diego, a win that sent New England to Super Bowl XLII. (That's 42 to you and me.)

In the Super Bowl, the 18-0 Patriots would not only be battling against the New York Giants, but also NFL history, as they tried to become only the second team in history to run the table from start through to the Super Bowl. The Pats were heavy favorites in this game, but the Giants were hot and took a 10-7 lead in the fourth quarter on an Eli Manning touchdown pass to David Tyree. As they had all season, the Patriots answered the bell. After an exchange of punts, New England went 80 yards in 12 plays with Tom Brady hitting Randy Moss from six yards out for the go ahead touchdown with 2:42 to play. New England led 14-10.

Ventrone played special teams the entire game, and as the Patriots prepared to kick off, the moment he had waited for his whole life was just around the corner.

"We knew that in order to have a chance to have an opportunity to win the game that we needed a big play," Ventrone remembers. "I approached the kick line and just tried to get down the field as fast as I could."

The ball came down into the hands of Giants return man Dominik Hixon at the three-yard-line.

"I beat my guy who was supposed to block me and I came around the end of the wedge and fortunately nobody peeled back to block me and I just hit the guy as hard as I could."

Ventrone unloaded on Hixon, burying him at the 17-yard line after just a 14-yard return, putting the Giants into a big hole. The undrafted, twice released, I-AA safety - who also overcame two major injuries - had just made the tackle of a lifetime in front of tens of thousands of people in Glendale, Arizona and tens of millions watching on TV worldwide. Not bad at all.

"After I made the hit, I mean I had so much adrenaline. Complete blur. I remember just jogging off the field and everybody just mauling me, mugging me as I was coming off the field, just congratulating me and I think everybody was really pumped up at that point. We thought that might have set up real good field position for our defense."

It was not to be, however. The Patriots' defense couldn't hold, and the Giants went the length of the field, with Eli Manning hitting Plaxico Burress for the game-winning score with just seconds remaining. Giants 17, Patriots 14.

"Obviously, you move on, but you know it comes to a point where that game will always be there. I'll never forget the feeling I had whenever we lost. It really is just unfortunate that we lost that game, because if we would have been able to go 19-0, we really would have been considered, probably the best team to ever play. It will definitely be tough to look at that one 20 years from now."

Ventrone had made an impression. So much so that the Patriots were looking for ways to get him more involved in 2008. And as it turns out, all of that work on the practice squad was going to pay dividends.

"Coach Belichick had actually told me that they were thinking about moving me to receiver in the spring and I wasn't really taking anything serious from it," Ventrone says, "but when the spring came around they actually did, they moved me to wide receiver. I was playing both receiver and safety, sitting in on both meetings and stuff."

Ventrone took to it. He actually tied for the team preseason lead with 9 catches and made the team. During the regular season, his action was limited to special teams, but he played in 15 of New England's 16 games in his first "full" season.

He was one of the Patriots' last cuts in 2009, but was reunited with Eric Mangini a third time as the now Cleveland Browns head coach quickly scooped him up. He literally was signed on a Wednesday and was covering kicks on Sunday.

So through it all, what kept him going when many, many players before him presented with half the obstacles would have said "enough"?

"My mentality in everything I do is to do everything to the best of my ability and to give maximum effort and never give up. It really is how I try to approach everything I do. Secondly, I love football. There are a few things that I love in my life and that's one of them and I'll do anything to keep playing."

Lift for Life

"That (Lift for Life) has become a part of what it means to be a Penn State football player. It's not quite black shoes, blue jersey, white helmet. But it's getting there."

– DAMONE JONES, CO-FOUNDER PSU "LIFT FOR LIFE"

I've learned about some really incredible charitable organizations and charitable events during my time in the media, but I can honestly say I don't think I've come across anything quite as impressive as the Penn State "Lift for Life". It's a summer weight lifting event held in State College that raises money for the Kidney Cancer Association. It's not just bench pressing and standard weight lifting activities, but also things like the giant tire flip and it's done in rapid-fire succession, pushing participants to their physical limits. What really makes this event stand out is that it was the brainchild of Penn State football players and to this day is run only by players. It also is now just one part of an organization that has grown into a million dollar non-profit called Uplifting Athletes, run by the man who helped start it all back in 2003, Scott Shirley.

The "Lift for Life" is really a shining example of how awful circumstances can bring out the best in people. Shirley's father Don was actually first diagnosed with kidney cancer back in 1993.

"At the time it was full encapsulated," Scott Shirley remembers. "It was found by mistake – they weren't necessarily looking for it.

THE SHIRLEY FAMILY

Don Shirley was the long time baseball coach at Mechanicsburg High School in Mechanicsburg, PA

But since it had not metastasized they were able to surgically remove his entire kidney. They did follow-up scans and after five years he was still quote, unquote cancer free so they gave him a clean bill of health."

Don Shirley really lived the life we all dream about. Father, husband, job he loved as English teacher and baseball coach at Mechanicsburg High School in Pennsylvania.

"He had over 400 wins," Shirley says. "He used to tease me he had more wins then Joe (Paterno), although Joe is finally catching him."

In 2002, Scott was a senior wide receiver at Penn State and as he was in the midst of the grind of a season, his life changed in an instant.

"I actually believe it was the week we were playing Iowa. I was on my way home from practice and I got a phone call from my mom and it was a call - you look at your phone, you see who it is and you know something is not right. Sure enough I picked up the phone and she was so emotional she couldn't even speak. So I pulled over into the Nittany Lion Inn parking lot and she was able to tell me that he had been diagnosed with kidney cancer. Advanced kidney cancer. Stage 4 metastatic renal cell carcinoma. He was told he would be lucky to see me graduate just six months later."

Despite the world-rocking news and grim diagnosis, Shirley was able to stay focused.

"My initial reaction was that he was going to be able to beat this because he lived a very healthy lifestyle – you hear about people beating cancer so I fully expected that he was going to be able to get through this. I was lucky enough that the coaches and my teachers let me go to different medical centers in the Mid-Atlantic region with my parents to try and find a course of action."

However, doctor after doctor told the Shirleys that nothing could be done for Don.

"In the spring (2003), we finally got in to see a highly respected institution and I thought it was like going to see the Wizard of Oz. I thought they were going to have the answer for us when we walked through the door and this was all going to be over."

But Scott and his family would get far less than that happy ending answer they were looking for.

"The head oncologist there didn't even close the door. He just stuck his head in and said the reality is there is nothing we can do. So that's when it hit me like a ton of bricks that something wasn't right and wasn't adding up."

On his way back to campus that day, Scott called the Kidney Cancer Association and learned that kidney cancer was one of the 7,000 rare diseases in the U.S. That means it affects less than 200,000 Americans. The relatively low number of people dealing with kidney cancer leads to a lack of funding for research, which leads to a lack of treatment options. This is kind of the flashpoint where the "Lift for Life" was born, as soon after that sobering visit with the oncologist, Shirley returned home to his apartment in State College.

"We knew Scott was going through something, but we didn't quite know what," remembers Damone Jones, Shirley's former roommate and teammate. "Then he came back home and was shaken for Scott and he kind of said it to us, 'Guys, this is what's going on with my dad and all this stuff about kidney cancer - nothing can be done.' And in typical Scott fashion, he had gone and learned everything he could about kidney cancer to try and help his family fight what was going on. He kind of looked at us and said something along the lines of feeling helpless that there is nothing anyone can do."

An offensive tackle, Jones says he had been kicking around ideas and ways to get himself, and the team, more involved in the community and this looked like the perfect opportunity to do just that. Shirley remembers that Jones didn't hesitate in stepping up.

"Damone shrugged his shoulders and said to me, 'Why don't we do something? We're Penn State football. If I wipe my ass sideways, it's on the front page of the paper. So lets take advantage of the position that we are in.'"

When Jones was kicking around ideas of how to help in the community, he targeted the team's summer lifting competition as a vehicle that could be used as the focus of their efforts. That concept continued as the focal point once Shirley and Jones started talking.

"We were a really good team," Jones says. "Because I'm a real big dreamer and he's a lot more meticulous than most people. So I would just throw out these wild ideas and these wild expectations and he was able to really manage them and make sure we were still working towards the goal."

Soon after these first conversations, another key player in the birth of the event would emerge in the person of offensive lineman Dave Costlow.

"When I joined the mix, we just started brainstorming. What are we going to do, how are we going to do it, how are we going to

The tire flip is one of the more interesting events at Penn State's "Lift for Life".

make an impact," Costlow remembers. "They wanted to do something and Damone in particular knew we could make an impact given the visibility that we have, the pull we had with so many fans as players. So the question was how do we capitalize on that, why would they listen to us and how do we engage them? So it all went from there, but it was an exciting couple of weeks when we started kicking around ideas."

"The three of us went to (Penn State Athletic Director) Tim Curley and pitched this idea and I have to give Tim Curley and Penn State a lot of credit for having the faith in us to organize this and letting us run with it. So he gave us his blessing," Shirley says.

Everybody was on board with the idea, but where do you go from here? Wanting to do something and pulling it off are two vastly different things. Shirley says things came together and the experience provided some great benefits they hadn't anticipated.

"The first one being the internship like experience. As we planned this first event, we sat around a table 6, 8 of us whatever and we say, 'Lets run a commercial on cable. Who knows how to do that?'

The "Lift for Life" has become a staple of the college football experience for Penn State players.

HARVEY LEVINE

Obviously none of us had ever done it before, but one of the guys was in an advertising class so we asked him. He had never done it, but he picked up the phone and called the cable company and said 'I'm a Penn State football player working on a charity project and this is what I'd like to do'. We reached out to people in the industry and they helped us apply what we had learned to the benefit of this cause."

Jones remembers a lot of discussion about how to get their message about what they are doing out to the people.

"We had our internal collection of people; teammates, classmates, people we met at Penn State. We were like, 'Hey, we can tell them and they'll donate and they'll do whatever we ask them to do because they are our friends and they love us.' But we realized that reach wasn't nearly what we thought it was. When we looked at it and it might be a collection of a thousand people between the three of us, of people we could really reach out to. We really started freaking out a little bit about what was possible from a marketing and outreach standpoint."

Jones credits longtime Penn State Sports Information Director Jeff Nelson with helping to guide them so they could get the right message about the "Lift for Life" to the right people. While Shirley, Jones and Costlow were the three main players this first year, Shirley says teammates were quick to step up and become a part of what they were doing.

"We really felt a paradigm shift in the locker room where this wasn't passive community service where we were just showing up with our jerseys on to get a picture taken to put in a newsletter. We had our sleeves rolled up, our hands were getting dirty and we were fully responsible – we had ownership of it and that gave us the ability to actively engage our teammates. It's a pretty powerful dynamic shift in the locker room when guys aren't saying 'do I have to do it' and instead are saying 'what can I do' or 'how can I help?' On top of that, when we did hold the event we learned that we did have the ability to mobilize the community. A couple hundred people showed up. We had a great time."

Shirley says it was exactly 100 days from his first conversation with Damone Jones to the initial "Lift for Life".

"We raised 13 thousand dollars."

It was given directly to the Kidney Cancer Association and they realized they were really on to something.

"That triggered higher expectations and we started talking at that point almost immediately about seeing this being a nationwide program benefiting this rare disease cause," Shirley says.

Jones actually says he was a little disappointed in the amount they raised at first, but that quickly faded as he realized the impact not just the event, but their efforts, made on people.

"We realized what we had created when people who we never heard of, people who had never talked to us before - the adoration they showed over what we had done. I think that's when we realized how special the thing we had just done was. And that was a pretty cool part of it."

"When we first started out it was 'Let's make a difference for Scott's dad,'" Costlow says, 'Let's make a difference for a cause that means something for us as a team.' As we went through the discovery process and realized that this is really affecting a bunch of teammates, you see that momentum starts to build. Then we start to piece together what are we really doing here. We are mobilizing our fan base, it's an opportunity for ourselves to learn job skills and to learn and then connect with patients and connect patients to our alumni and we started to talk about all these pieces and you could start to see this vague 'perfect storm' forming. No one was obviously thinking 'okay this thing is going to go national or this is going to be a big organiza-tion', but I think we kind of realized there's a lot of really good build-ing blocks here. If we could figure out how to just fit them together I think there is a lot we could do with the organization at Penn State and obviously being able to connect to other universities."

It was quite obvious that the "Lift for Life" was here to stay. An-other example of the impact of what they were doing was having on people came following the second event in 2004, which raised $40,000. Shirley says as he, Costlow and Carrie Konosky, a member of the Penn State dance team who became an integral part of the event that second year, were preparing thank you letters for donors they started discussing how they had never actually met anyone from the Kidney Cancer Association.

"It was a Thursday night we had this conversation. It just so happened that the only time that we were all three available was that weekend," Shirley remembers.

A quick call to the KCA revealed that this was actually the week-end of their biggest patient conference and while the three would be welcomed with open arms, the small staff might not be able to spend as much time as they would like with the Penn State contingent. It was quickly determined that it was worth the risk and Shirley, Costlow and Konosky rented a car and headed out to Chicago, where the As-sociation is headquartered. Shirley says that about an hour outside of the Windy City they got a call from the Director of Development for the Kidney Cancer Association, asking if they were still coming.

"We said, 'Absolutely.' She said, 'Great, our keynote speaker just cancelled – would you mind filling in for him?' The valet meets us at the curb. They usher us right up on stage. We still hadn't met anybody yet. We managed to put together a little power point presentation in the car and walked up on stage, introduced ourselves, showed a little video and went through this little power point. We were interrupted three times in a matter of 5-10 minutes for standing ovations. Because the people in that room, not just the patients, but the family members, even the doctors and researchers that have dedicated their lives to kidney cancer all live in a world where they are constantly reminded that what they do isn't big enough or important to get attention. And the three of us walked in off the street from a college campus 10 hours away and said, 'This is what were doing because its important to us.' And it was really kind of a magical moment in the history of our organization and theirs. That's something they still talk about as being a critical point for them."

"I think that's what really helped us all get hooked," Konosky says. "Being able to meet more patients than just Scott's dad and see what an impact we made with them."

The whole "Lift for Life" experience would really make an impact on Konosky who actually now works for the Kidney Cancer Association as their current Director of Development and Public Affairs.

I described the "Lift" itself earlier, but Costlow gives us a first-hand breakdown of what makes this event special. It should be noted that just about everyone I have ever spoken to about the intensity of the workout has used the word 'sadistic' in one form or another.

"It is definitely the most intense thing that I have ever done athletically in terms of total commitment for the amount of period of time and the multitude of exercises and the complete sheer exhaustion. There is the physical part that people can observe and they can see guys struggling. But the guys who have always done well in that event are the guys that can prepare themselves and mentally can convince themselves that 'I'm not tired' and ignore the pain and ignore the queasiness and really try to focus on what you can do physically. I think that's the one thing that I think is difficult for people to appreciate if they've never gone through the lift is kind of the mental focus it takes to not completely crumble."

Prior to this second "Lift for Life", a WAY scaled down version of the event was held for us media types to take part in. I made up for not being able to finish by booting in a trash can which Dave Costlow was nice enough to hold without asking any questions. However, I also had the honor to meet Don Shirley. At this time, if you didn't know any better, you would have had no idea cancer was or ever had been an issue in his life. A lifelong Phillies fan, we talked about the team and that summer I was able to send him a Phils media guide and he in turn sent me a wonderful thank you note, that to this day I still have. Even though that would turn out to be the only time I would meet him in person, he was one of those people that you felt like you had known all your life.

"People wanted to live up to his expectations of him. I think that's one of the things that I've learned from talking to other people about him and as a father, a motto he lived by was to prepare his children for the path, not the path for his children. I think that there is a lot of that in who I am today," Shirley says.

A kidney cancer specialist in 2003 had put Don on an immunotherapy, to try and boost his immune system while also taking out as much of the cancer as they could surgically.

"So they did a very intense surgery because the tumor had grown to touch vital organs and it was starting to impede his vena cava," Shirley says. "So they had to remove two ribs and go through his diaphragm to remove this tumor. Then they surgically repaired the diaphragm and actually I don't know what they did with the ribs, but when he came out of that 6 weeks later they removed half of his lung because it had metastasized to his lung. From that point he lived a pretty normal life again for two years."

Well enough to take part in that media "Lift for Life" event and start jogging again.

"To the point where he had jogged five miles before he had gone back for his first check-up and the doctor told him that it would be ok if he wanted to start walking again. My dad said, 'Well, I just ran five miles, is that ok?' And the doctor about fell over."

However in the spring of 2005, Shirley's father took a turn for the worse with the cancer spreading to his liver. The next several months would see a steady decline in his condition.

"The liver filters toxins to the brain so he was starting to get delirious. The lucid moments became less frequent. If you can imagine Alzheimer's, it was kind of like that. He really would get confused. I remember my birthday (October 9th) when my sister was on her knees in front of him in the Lay-z-boy trying to get him to eat a piece of cake and explaining to him why we were doing this. That was the hardest part, seeing him losing his mind like that."

During this time, Shirley says they were able to get his father into the compassionate phase of a new drug for kidney cancer, and soon after Scott's birthday they went to see the doctor.

"They told us that the tumor had actually stabilized because of this new treatment. And I remember walking out in the hallway of this hospital with my mom, and we were talking and the thought actually crossed my mind of him coaching baseball again that spring. Whether it was denial or optimism or what, I had a moment where I was convinced he was going to be coaching again within 6 months. So I never really acknowledged the end until the end."

The end would come on October 17th, 2005.

"I had been bedside for 5 or 6 days, pretty much around the clock. But I went out on the afternoon of the 17th to buy a bicycle because I wanted to start to ride a bike," Shirley remembers. "My intent was to train to ride with Lance Armstrong - he was leading a (cancer) ride from San Diego to DC that was sponsored by a pharmaceutical company. So I went out that afternoon to get fitted for a bike because I was going to get into biking to be a part of that ride. It was while I left that he passed away. My sister called me to tell me the news so that I wasn't surprised when I came home. It was very difficult because I wanted to be there and I had just excused myself for that reason and that's when we lost him. And then, I don't know if its "Murphy's Law" or whatever but that ride with Lance never happened again. They created some different events because the pharmaceutical company backed out of the sponsorship so they cancelled that ride."

When it came time for Shirley's life to be celebrated, Scott says his father's legacy was crystallized.

"At his funeral all these different circles of people from his life came together. It was amazing to see the impact that he had on all them and as a father, as a member of a family being a brother, a husband; he was great in that role. He was equally great in his role as a coach, in his role as an educator, in his role as a person of faith. But never before had I seen all those people together and it was really inspiring for me to see that throughout his life, he had a similar impact on all those people just as he did us."

Even after the passing of the man whose battle led to its start, the "Lift for Life" would continue to grow and Jones says he realized how far it had come during a post-graduation visit.

"When I went back in 2006, it was the first "Lift for Life" I was able to make it back for. Now there were bleachers, thousands of people showing up. It was a full-on event. I'm getting chills talking about it now. But that was one of the coolest damn things I ever seen."

The event was getting so big at Penn State that it was becoming apparent that this indeed was a concept that needed to move beyond State College.

"We met David Wozniak (Vice President and Head of Advertising and Brand Development at Lincoln Financial Group) and he is now a member of our board," Shirley says. "He helped us write a business plan the year following my dad's death because we felt like the chapter at Penn State was to the point where we could reproduce it. Dave got involved with us and helped us write that business plan to take that next step. And without his insight and his contribution I don't know if we would be where we are right now."

Wozniak, a 1986 Penn State alum, says he learned about the event in one of its first years, reading a story on it by one of the best Penn State writers out there, Mark Brennan.

"It was just one of those stories that really hit me. It caused me to send a check. I made a donation and a short while later I got a thank you back from Scott. He and I just started some correspondence and I said, 'Hey, this is what I do, if there something I can do to help you let me know' and then one thing led to another and it's just taken off from there."

Wozniak says the way the Penn State event has grown has really impressed him.

"They learn from what they've done in the past and they are able to apply new thinking to it; they continue to shape it and evolve it and I think through those transitions that its really helped Penn State add another tradition to a long storied football program."

That tradition began to spread, as the "Lift for Life" would soon become one aspect in the non-profit organization "Uplifting Athletes."

"The mission of Uplifting Athletes is to align college football with rare diseases and raise them as a national priority through advocacy, education, research and outreach," Shirley says. "So we see ourselves now as being what the American Cancer Society is to cancer patients; we see ourselves as that organization for rare disease patients, and being synonymous with college football and creating an experience for the football players through their involvement that is life changing."

Shirley would soon leave his successful career as an engineer in Washington, D.C. to become the executive director.

"He busted his hump," Jones says. "The kid, he worked so hard to hone his craft as an engineer and to be the best young engineer in the country. That is what he wanted to be. And he was doing it. When Scott told me he was going to leave his job to help Uplifting Athletes become a more sustainable organization and make sure that the impact is even greater than it already is, I think that was the first time I realized that this initial vision of an army of football players doing good across the country, that was the first time I thought, 'Wow this thing's really going to happen.'"

Uplifting Athletes now has official chapters at Penn State, Ohio State, Boston College, Maryland and Colgate, each working to benefit the fight against a rare disease. Some twenty other schools, Shirley says, are in various stages of development. While Boston College and Colgate both have lift events similar to Penn State, Ohio State and Maryland use a video game challenge as their centerpiece event.

"It is so critical to us through our expansion that two things re-main consistent - that each chapter is run by the players, and that each chapter benefits a rare disease that is relevant to them so that they can have that same experience and that same impact," Shirley says. "To be frank, we are never going to raise enough money to cure 7000 different diseases. But if we can make rare diseases "popular", if we can make them mainstream, if we can make them matter, then other people will want to get involved and do things independently to start to address the problems."

As for the continuing battle against kidney cancer, when Don Shirley was diagnosed in the fall of 2002, there was only one FDA approved treatment. Konosky says the playing field is now starting to level out.

"In the last seven years, we have six new drugs for kidney cancer patients. So while we still don't have a cure, these drugs are giving patients hope that their lives can extend and they have more times with their families and hopefully during that time there will be something else that comes along that may be the cure. I know when we started and when Scott's dad got sick there really wasn't anything for them and they were told, 'Just go home and enjoy the time that you have left.' Now it's a totally different story for patients."

Jones is a member of the Uplifting Athletes board and proud of what he helped begin.

"I had visions of leaving a legacy of great offensive line play and being drafted and being All- American and All-Big Ten and my career didn't pan out there. But knowing that I was part of a group that left a legacy that extends beyond what goes on on Saturdays - that actually helps people. Knowing that I played a part in something that maximizes the potential of sport, that's what I'm proudest of."

"Like anything, there is a great deal of pride in knowing that you were kind of there at the outset," Costlow says. "And there is also almost a level of gratitude and almost a sense of humility that there have been people who have stepped in and done things and carried it on and really created what lives today."

Shirley, who has now dedicated his career to the battle against kidney cancer and all rare diseases, is quick to incorporate his personal journey over the past several years into the big picture.

"This isn't about my dad and it certainly isn't about me," Shirley says. "It's about what we have learned from his situation. I never really took a step back and looked at it as a coping mechanism or a source of hope. But it's indisputable that what we do is inspiring all these people with hope and that's one of the best parts of what I'm doing right now."

However, dad is always with him.

"I miss him like crazy and I think he would be awfully proud of what we've done."

Former Villanova kicker Joe Marcoux donated blood-forming cells to a patient in need in 2006.

Be The Match:
Andy Talley

"It's hard and rare to find an individual who connects to a cause and stays with it forever. That's what Andy Talley has done. It's an amazing thing to me. Just amazing."

– SUEANNE PAPROCKI, OF THE
"BE THE MATCH" NATIONAL MARROW DONOR PROGRAM

I have done a story about the Villanova football bone marrow testing drive several times over the years. And every time I would talk to Head Coach Andy Talley about the program that he created and has spearheaded for nearly two decades, I couldn't help but notice the passion in his voice and the pride on his face. Now usually when I come across someone in the world of sports who has become immersed in an important charitable cause, it's because it is something that has touched them or their family on a very personal level. I must admit that for several years I just assumed Coach Talley was so determined to get people to join the bone marrow registry because he had had a friend or relative that was not able to find a donor. The fact that he took on the cause simply because he felt it needed taking on makes the work even more special.

The long road that has seen thousands of names added to the National Bone Marrow Donor Registry began one day in the early 90s, when the longtime Villanova football coach was listening to a radio show.

"An oncologist came on and said, 'People die every day because we don't have enough people on the bone marrow registry.' So all these people were dying and I said, 'I've got 90 players on my team that are healthy.'"

So in 1992, he held his first drive to get people on the registry, bringing on board all of his players, friends of the football program and students. This continued over the years. Every player that came through Villanova would get entered into the registry in the spring, Coach Talley doing his best to spread the word about the importance of the registry and to add more and more names.

What makes it so important?

Sueanne Paprocki, with the "Be the Match" National Marrow Donor Program, gives us the facts about marrow transplants.

"Usually the people who need these transplants have leukemia, lymphoma, types of blood cancer. The only way for a cure is to have a transplant. First place they look for a match is family, but about 70% do not have a match."

That's where the registry comes in.

"We are matching human leukocyte antigens, markers on your immune system. And we have to have a perfect match."

Paprocki says that about 10,000 people in the US need a marrow transplant per year but, on the average, only four to five thousand transplants are being performed because of a lack of matches. That math speaks volumes as to the importance of increasing the number of people on the registry. In addition, diversity is an issue, as you generally find matches within you own ethnicity or race group.

"The chance of a Caucasian getting a bone marrow transplant used to be 1 in 100,000. Now it's 1 in 60,000," Talley says. "One in a million for an African-American, Asian or Hispanic. So in other words, if you're Asian, Hispanic or African American, the chances of getting a bone marrow transplant are slim to none."

But this is another area where involving college campuses and athletes could help make a real difference, as they both tend to be pretty diverse.

"I was motivated by the fact that my 90 players could actually help someone save a life," Talley says.

The concept of a bone marrow transplant, even just getting on the registry to possibly provide one, can sound intimidating. But the process to get registered is really incredibly simple. As Talley quickly points out, all it is some paperwork and "a simple cheek swab."

In the mid-90s, a Villanova player was a match for someone who needed a transplant and that player went ahead with the donation process. The patient unfortunately did not survive and the player has asked that his identity be kept private. He would, however, not be the last Wildcat to try to save a life.

In the spring of 2006, Villanova players took part in that year's drive to get names entered into the registry. One of the players getting his cheek swabbed and filling out the necessary paperwork was kicker Joe Marcoux, who had made 3 of 4 field goals and 17 of 20 extra points during his freshman season in the fall. The Campbell Hall, NY native says he really didn't give the registry much thought once the drive was over. That is, until a few months later in the summer of '06, when he was contacted and told he was a potential match for someone in dire need of a bone marrow transplant.

"I didn't hesitate. Went right for it, said yes. I told Coach Talley afterwards and said I already gave them the go ahead."

Marcoux says this was just the first step in the process.

"They call you and confirm and then you go in for further testing to make sure that you are the best match for this person. So you go in for blood testing and all that stuff. And then you get another call saying you are the match. That's probably about a month after you get the first result."

Marcoux was indeed a perfect match. The identities of those in need are kept confidential. Even the person donating the bone marrow is not told who it will benefit, with the exception of a few basic facts. So all he knew was that he would be helping a 53-year-old woman who was struggling with leukemia.

Once all of the screening and paperwork was in order, the 2006 season had come and gone. On December 1st, Marcoux was set to undergo the procedure. There are actually two ways you can donate. One sees liquid marrow taken out of your bone through a surgical procedure and the other is a collection of stem cells from the blood stream – which is what Marcoux would be doing.

"With stem cells you have to get shots for a week before you actually donate," Marcoux says. "So that's where it really kind of sets in. You have to get two shots a day and it's not an easy shot; it makes you feel groggy, and it makes you achy. So the reality sets in once you're in that process."

Hahnemann Hospital in Philadelphia would be the place Marcoux would undergo the actual procedure.

"You get there early in the morning, you register. You sit there, they give you some more shots and basically you sit in a chair. I was there for about seven hours and it's just a needle in one arm and one needle in the top of the other arm. And it's just a long process where you can't move, you can't do anything."

And with that, Marcoux had taken the extraordinary step of doing all he could to try and save the life of a complete stranger.

"I think it was big for me because it was around the holidays and just to give somebody another chance. It felt like you accomplished something with your life."

Then in the spring, Marcoux was contacted once again and told that the patient he was a match for needed another transplant. Without hesitation he started the process to donate all over again. However, right before he was to go in for the actual procedure, he was told that she had taken a turn for the worse and that the transplant was no longer an option. She passed soon after. Even though Marcoux had never met her - didn't even know her name - they were connected and her death touched him.

"I did feel sadness a little bit, but I looked at it more on the positive side as I gave them so many more months with their family and I did all I could. Yeah I didn't know them, but I gave all I could to somebody who needed it."

Would he do it again if called?

"Absolutely. Without a doubt."

So what started

VILLANOVA UNIVERSITY ATHLETICS

Villanova Head Football Coach Andy Talley has worked to get thousands of people added to the National Bone Marrow Registry.

in the early 90s by a football coach listening to a radio show has now turned into a nationwide crusade. Dozens of college football teams across the country, including virtually every one from the Delaware Valley, now hold their own bone marrow registry drives. The goal is to add thousands of new names to the national registry every year. The teams hold the events to coincide with their spring practices or their spring games. And those events are beginning to bear fruit. At the end of the 2009 season, Matt Hoffman, a defensive end at Division III Rowan University in Glassboro, New Jersey, underwent the same procedure as Marcoux to try and save the life of a 52-year-old man suffering from non-Hodgkin lymphoma.

"It's pretty easy to ask a football coach, 'Hey, will you help me do something that will save a life,'" Talley says, "Every football coach is going to say, 'Yeah.'"

And needless to say, the coach's passion for this cause isn't going to subside anytime soon.

"What I need to know is that we actually saved somebody's life and I just know we have. I'll just never know about it. But I'll know there is some mother, some father, some child who is going to have his mom and dad. Or some mom and dad who are going to have their child for the rest of their lives because of the work that we did.

Paprocki says she is really in awe at what Talley has done.

"This isn't just someone who sees kind of a nice thing, comes out and does it on drive, puts their heart and soul into it and then disappears into their busy life. This is a person who saw this, made a commitment, and hasn't stopped with that commitment and continues that commitment. This is a football coach who said, 'I need to do something. I need to step up to the plate. I need to be the one'. And when you think about this, he really became the one."

For more information on how you can join the National Bone Marrow Donor Registry or to learn more about the urgent need for donors, please visit www.marrow.org.

Dan Cepero

"I mean we ribbed Danny right after the fact. We said, 'Where was that when you were at Penn?'"

– PENN SOCCER COACH RUDY FULLER

Dan Cepero was an All-Ivy soccer player during his time at the University of Pennsylvania. Good enough that he caught the attention of pro scouts, in 2007 he was taken by the New York Red Bulls in the 4th round of the Major League Soccer (MLS) Supplemental Draft. After a year and a half of training and playing in developmental leagues, Cepero finally got the call to the big time on October 18th, 2008 when he made his MLS debut against the Columbus Crew at the Meadowlands. Not only did he play, but Cepero also scored a goal in a 3-1 Red Bulls win.

Wait . . . did I mention Cepero is a goalie? Darn. I always do that. It's why I'm a terrible joke teller.

The road to this magical moment actually started rather humbly, as Cepero was not actively recruited at Penn. As Quakers Head Coach Rudy Fuller puts it, he was a "glorified walk-on." The Quakers had been in contact with him and, the summer after his senior year of high-school, Cepero, who had already been admitted to and decided to attend Penn, sent a video of some of his highlights to the Penn coaching staff.

"When we got back to the office on a full-time basis and were trying to catch-up on all our mail and videos, my assistant at the

PENN ATHLETICS

Dan Cepero working on his form during his days at Penn.

time, Bob Butehorn (now the head coach at Florida Gulf Coast), had popped his video in," Fuller remembers, "and this is maybe second week in August, so we were coming into preseason the following week. He popped this video in and then he threw it over to me and said, 'You should take a look at this kid, he's coming and he's pretty good.' And I did the same and we ended up calling Danny and I essentially said, 'Do you think you could make it down for preseason here at Penn next week?' And he was like, 'Absolutely Coach, I'll be there.'"

From there, Cepero developed into that All-Ivy goalie. He eventually rewrote the Quakers record book, finishing with 23 career shutouts between the pipes. That success eventually caught the Red Bulls' eye.

Cepero found out a few days before that Saturday night game with Columbus that he would be making his debut, so he had some time to think about things.

"I think the nerves kind of subsided by Saturday. I was just more anxious, I think, to kind of just get on the field and get playing."

This game, the regular season home finale, was huge for the Red Bulls, as they were fighting for their playoff lives. But Cepero, making his debut in a game of this magnitude, wasn't necessarily how the home team drew this one up.

The Baldwin, NY native had been on loan from the Red Bulls to the Harrisburg City Islanders of USL-2 for much of the season. And he probably wouldn't have suited up at all for the Red Bulls - save the fact that starting goalie Jon Conway was suspended after testing positive for performance-enhancing substances prior to the game with Columbus. So controversy, critical match, playoffs on the line - go get 'em kid.

"Once the whistle blew, it was just a matter of settling in and getting used to the environment. With 18 some thousand fans out there - the noise gets you. Kind of takes you by surprise," Cepero says. "But I would say probably about 10 minutes in when you get your first touch on the ball - you realize, 'Hey I can do this. I've been here before. I've played soccer my whole life.'"

Cepero made his first save late in the first half with a diving stop to keep the match scoreless heading into the locker room. New York would strike first in the 48th minute, only to see Columbus tie things up a few minutes later. The Red Bulls had taken a 2-1 lead late in the second half when a foul occurred just outside Cepero's box. The goalie lined up for a direct kick in the 83rd minute.

"I mean it's just something that you do day in and day out. It makes more sense for the goalkeeper to just take the kick and get his defenders to step up - rather than have a defender take it," Cepero explains. "I was trying to play it ideally to one of our players, hoping they would be able to control it. I had no intention of doing what I did."

The blast traveled some 60 yards in the air, then took a big bounce about twenty yards from the goal, which fooled Crew goal-keeper Andy Gruenebaum, who never got a handle on it, and it ended up in the back of the net.

"I didn't realize what had happened," Cepero admitted, "that it had bounced over and went in – until my defenders come running after me and I'm just like, 'What's going on?' I see the net move, couldn't really see it, didn't really know what was going and I had to ask them as they came to me and were celebrating. I was like, 'What just happened?'"

What happened is Cepero became the first goalie in MLS history to score a goal. He also put the finishing touches on a 3-1 win that would spark a Red Bulls run, not only into the playoffs, but all the way through to the MLS Cup Final.

The same night Cepero made history, his alma mater was in Hanover, New Hampshire for a critical Ivy League match with Dartmouth. The Quakers won 1-0 and Coach Fuller remembers that postgame fondly.

"When we got back to the bus the only thing anyone wanted to find out was how New York was doing because Danny was in goal. Obviously, our team was in a good mood and there was a lot of energy. We get back to the bus, everybody turns on their cell phones, trying to get an update on the score and how the game went and somebody yelled out, 'Red Bulls winning 3-1.' There was a huge cheer and music was blaring and guys were high-fiving and it was just a great night for our program."

Fuller says his team continued to dig for more detail about Cepero's debut.

"Seconds later somebody else yells out, 'Holy crap, Cepero scored a goal.' And the bus literally went silent as guys tried to digest it. The first instinct was it's got to be a mistake, a misprint or whatever. And everybody was looking around and sure enough there he was on the scoresheet. It was just a great night."

Cepero was by no means a one-hit wonder. Granted, he didn't score again, but Conway was done for the season and so the Red Bulls turned the goalkeeping chores over to him and he was between the pipes for the entire postseason run. He allowed just one goal total in three playoff matches before Columbus took revenge on him, beating him three times in a 3-1 win in the MLS Cup Final.

While he's proud of making history, Cepero wants to be known for more than just being the goalie that scored.

"It's not something that I harp on too much. It was a great moment in what I hope to be a longer career."

But he says it was something that he was asked about quite regularly during his time in New York.

"You know, I think I would have to go with weekly," Cepero admits. "I think a lot of the time you're meeting different fans for the first time so you're not seeing the same ones where you can kind of address that and move on. When you're bouncing around and going to appearances and signing autographs and going to different clubs, you know when you meet new people, it's the one thing that sticks in their minds because it doesn't happen every day on a soccer field."

No. No it doesn't.

Dave Micahnik

"You never know how many years you'll get breathing, let alone fencing, but I expected it to be long term. I wanted it to be a career."

If you took an informal sample of the greatest coaches in many sports, you'd probably be surprised to see that many times they were not standouts performers in said sport. In fact, some of baseball's greatest managers never played in the Major Leagues and some top NFL and college football coaches were reserves, at best. Knowing that makes you appreciate even more what longtime Penn fencing coach Dave Micahnik achieved. He not only led the Quakers for 35 years until his retirement in 2009, but also put together a phenomenal career as a competitor in his own right.

Now before we get too far, how about a primer on fencing, because I think it's one of those sports that a lot of people (ok, me) are fascinated watching at the Olympics every four years, but really don't know anything about. Well, I can't help helping, so here we go. First, Micahnik describes the real essence of fencing.

"It's a combat sport. There is no extra credit for impact and certainly no danger because weapons are not sharp and you wear protective clothing that's designed to make the sport quite safe."

The main object is to score more points than your opponent during the course of a bout, using one of three weapons: epée, foil or

Longtime Penn Fencing Coach Dave Micahnik as a US Olympian

saber. The weapons are different weights, which is what sets them apart, along with the scoring used when each weapon is involved. And, according to the USA Fencing website, fencing is one of just four sports to be included in every modern Olympic games since the first in 1896.

For a man who dedicated his life to the sport, Micahnik got a bit of a late start, not taking up the epée until he arrived on the campus of the University of Pennsylvania as a freshman in 1955.

"I didn't even play any sports at all until I got to college. I wasn't very athletic at that time and it was just a matter of curiosity. I had heard about it (fencing), but didn't know a thing about it. And I said let me try that and see. I'll learn something about it, I'll get cut from the team and that will be the end of that. And I didn't get cut."

Micahnik would start his career on the Penn freshman team.

"Many schools had newcomers on their freshmen team who were learning to fence while in college, so it wasn't that much of a disadvantage right away. I started to have some success with it and there is kind of a feedback loop between motivation and success. The more you do well, the more you want to do and it just keeps going around. I just started outsweating people, and was able to make a fairly good career out of it."

That may be the understatement of the season. Micahnik would quickly move up to the varsity team and develop into a premier fencer, making his name on the national stage just a few years after taking up the sport. The epée would become his main weapon and, in 1960, he would take part in the National Championships, with a shot at the Olympic Games on the line.

"I got to the Final 8 of the National Championships and said, 'If I win a couple bouts, I'm on the team.' Then (Penn coach) Maestro (Lajos) Csiszar said, 'If you don't get a medal you won't get to fence the individuals. So I said, 'Well, then I better win every possible bout.'"

Micahnik did just that, putting it all together, winning all seven bouts in the final round and clinching the National Championship.

"The competition was over at about maybe 11 that night, but somewhere between 1 and 2 in the morning, after everybody else had cleared out — it was in the ballroom of the old Commodore Hotel in New York — I was still walking around in a daze coming to grips with the reality of it."

The 1960 Olympic Games in Rome would be the first of three in which Micahnik would compete. He would also represent the US in 1964 in Tokyo and in 1968 in Mexico City after finishing second in the National Championships both years. In all three Games he would advance out of the first round of pool play, but be eliminated in the second.

"In my naivete, I thought if I really fenced my best game, I'd really have a shot. I found out that experience is a big deal," Micahnik remembers. "I had some good bouts and did well in some situations. As I've said a couple of times, I was good enough to beat pretty much anybody, but in a situation like that you have to beat them all in one day. And I couldn't beat enough people in one day."

But the Olympics are about more than the competition; they are about representing your country and memories and experiences that most of us can only dream about. One such memory for Micahnik occurred in '64, a chance run-in with a guy who had a pretty good run as an Olympian. His name was Al Oerter, the greatest Olympic discus thrower ever. Oerter would win gold in the discus in 56, 60, 64 and 68. Micahnik would cross paths with him in the trainer's room.

"I was having some stiffness in my back, and I went to get it loosened up. He was on the next table getting an ice massage on his chest because of some torn cartilage. I said, 'Hi there, I'm Dave.' He said, 'Hi, I'm Al.' I said, 'What's going on?' and he told me that he had a torn cartilage and he was being treated, but he that he couldn't train."

Micahnik asked him how he planned to compete if he couldn't train.

"He explained the way your preliminary round distances carried up to the finals and said, 'I'm going to go out there and I'm going to throw it as hard as I can and as far as I can and let them try and catch me'. I said, 'Isn't that likely to tear (the cartilage) again? He said, 'If it tears, it tears. This is the Olympics! You're supposed to die for this

Dave Micahnik spent 35 Years as the Penn Quakers Fencing Coach

one.' Sure enough, Oerter let it fly on his second throw, tore the cartilage again, and nobody caught him. He did tell that story, I think, in a book. I know I've heard the story in interviews and I've heard it quoted. Nobody ever says whom he said it to. He probably didn't even know who he was talking to; I was just the guy at the next table."

Another moment in Tokyo helped crystallize the Olympic experience for Micahnik, and to this day he gets emotional when recalling it.

"I was in a taxi in Tokyo. The cabby, who spoke minimal English, referred to me as "senshu," but I didn't understand what that word meant. I said, 'What is it?' and he said, 'Champion.' I said, 'I'm not a champion. I didn't win.' He said, 'You compete in Olympic Games, you are a champion.' He had it right."

Micahnik just missed the Olympic team in 1972 literally "by a touch" and then fell just short of the National Finals in 1973.

"I said ok, its time to move on. I'm not getting better and when you're not getting better it's time to see if there's a new direction.

That's exactly the time that a position opened up at Penn and I applied for it. I was hired as a kind of a recreation assistant and a de facto assistant coach to Maestro Csiszar."

When Csiszar retired in 1974, Micahnik took over the program. This would be the beginning of a head-coaching career at Penn that would see hundreds of wins for both his men's and women's teams. But of course you never forget your first.

"I didn't quite know how to manage a team, to get them ready, as a rookie coach. We were fencing Rutgers and we went to 13-13. 14 wins it. In the last bout, I had a freshman that had lost his first two bouts and I gave him a vote of confidence before the bout. I said, 'Jack, I know you can do this; you're in this spot because I wanted you here.' He said, 'Ok, but let me do it my way.' I said, 'You do it the way you see fit.' It went to a 4-4 tie, overtime. Next touch wins. Other guy attacks him, he doesn't defend himself, he counter-attacks, the other guy misses, Jack hits him, we win the meet. It wasn't like it was a random action; he had set it up. You can only get one shot at winning the first one."

Micahnik would start with just the men's team, but soon after taking over, he would get the reins of both programs. His Penn teams would maintain an incredibly high level of excellence, and when he retired in 2009, he had put together a combined men's and women's coaching record of 722-210. As you can imagine, a coaching career like that would have more than its share of special moments and teams.

"In 1978 we had a dominant foil team. They had been winning the IFA foil championship for a couple of years in a row so the foil was solid; saber was a combination of experienced fencers and hope for the best with the third man. The epée team was sound. The IFA's is scored by cumulative bouts, match by match, weapon by weapon and you add them up. By the end of the competition, we had blown away the field and broken the record for the most victories in the tournament. The men's team just cruised, won the Ivy's, won the

IFA's. We went on to have a couple of All-Americans that year from the men's team."

Micahnik would also be at the helm of two National Championship teams, one men's and one women's. The men's title was in 1981.

"It was still one man in each weapon as the format at that time and you added up the bout victories to see what your team score was. The men scored a 1st, a 3rd and a 9th and we won the NCAA Championships by a couple of bouts and of course that was spectacular. It was in beautiful downtown Kenosha, Wisconsin, University of Wisconsin-Parkside campus."

A few years later, in 1986, Micahnik's women would claim the top prize.

"They breezed through a USFA collegiate tournament in January, didn't have a close match and I thought, 'This is good.' As the season progressed, they did not have a close meet. It got to the point where I could give them a scoresheet and say, 'Come back and tell me how much you won by.' I could just stay with the men, and the women would just cruise. That went on all the way up through and including the NCAA Championships. They were just so dominant."

Micahnik would have not just coaching success from a team standpoint during his time at Penn, but he would also coach individuals to great heights. During his three and a half decades as head coach, he produced 44 All-Americans (29 men and 15 women) and 90 All-Ivy selections (61 men and 29 women). In addition, 32 Quakers competed internationally as members of United States national teams under Micahnik's tutelage.

His success led him to be inducted into the United States Fencing Association Hall of Fame as a member of its 2008 class. He's also been honored with membership into the Philadelphia Jewish Sports Hall of Fame and the University of Pennsylvania Athletic Hall of Fame.

He announced his decision to retire in April of 2009.

"There's no such thing as an actual right time. There's a time when you feel like you have done what you can accomplish and you become your own hard act to follow in many ways. I want to move on to another phase of my life to enjoy going places and seeing things and doing some things I haven't had time to do before. So it just seemed like a good moment."